W9-AMV-375

Visual Texture on Fabric

Create Stunning Art Cloth with Water-Based Resists

Lisa Kerpoe

C&T PUBLISHING

Text and Photography copyright © 2012 by Lisa Kerpoe

Photography and Artwork copyright © 2012 by C&T Publishing, Inc.

Publisher: **Amy Marson**

Creative Director: **Gailen Runge**

Editor: **Lynn Koolish**

Technical Editor: **Mary E. Flynn**

Cover Designer: **April Mostek**

Book Designer: **Rose Sheifer**

Production Coordinators: **Jenny Davis** and **Jessica Jenkins**

Production Editor: **Alice Mace Nakanishi**

How-to photography by Michael Attwood, Attwood Studio; other photography by Christina Carty-Francis and Diane Pedersen of C&T Publishing, Inc., unless otherwise noted

Published by C&T Publishing, Inc., P.O. Box 1456, Lafayette, CA 94549

All rights reserved. No part of this work covered by the copyright hereon may be used in any form or reproduced by any means—graphic, electronic, or mechanical, including photocopying, recording, taping, or information storage and retrieval systems—without written permission from the publisher. The copyrights on individual artworks are retained by the artists as noted in *Visual Texture on Fabric*. These designs may be used to make items only for personal use or donation to nonprofit groups for sale or for display only at events, provided the following credit is included on a conspicuous label: Designs copyright © 2012 by Lisa Kerpoe from the book *Visual Texture on Fabric* from C&T Publishing, Inc. Permission for all other purposes must be requested in writing from C&T Publishing, Inc.

Attention Teachers: C&T Publishing, Inc., encourages you to use this book as a text for teaching. Contact us at 800-284-1114 or www.ctpub.com for lesson plans and information about the C&T Creative Troupe.

We take great care to ensure that the information included in our products is accurate and presented in good faith, but no warranty is provided nor are results guaranteed. Having no control over the choices of materials or procedures used, neither the author nor C&T Publishing, Inc., shall have any liability to any person or entity with respect to any loss or damage caused directly or indirectly by the information contained in this book. For your convenience, we post an up-to-date listing of corrections on our website (www.ctpub.com). If a correction is not already noted, please contact our customer service department at ctinfo@ctpub.com or at P.O. Box 1456, Lafayette, CA 94549.

Trademark (™) and registered trademark (®) names are used throughout this book. Rather than use the symbols with every occurrence of a trademark or registered trademark name, we are using the names only in the editorial fashion and to the benefit of the owner, with no intention of infringement.

Library of Congress Cataloging-in-Publication Data

Kerpoe, Lisa, 1961-

Visual texture on fabric : create stunning art cloth with water-based resists / Lisa Kerpoe.

p. cm.

ISBN 978-1-60705-447-4 (soft cover)

1. Dyes and dyeing, Domestic. 2. Dyes and dyeing--Textile fibers. 3. Resist-dyed textiles. I. Title.

TT853.K39 2012

667'.2--dc23

2011034030

Printed in China

10 9 8 7 6 5 4 3 2 1

Acknowledgments

It is difficult to acknowledge all those who helped make this book possible. People from my past who encouraged me as an artist are just as significant as those who provided guidance and technical support on this project.

My husband deserves much of the thanks. He believed in me fourteen years ago when I quit a corporate career to fulfill my dream. I would have abandoned my art many times over the past fourteen years without the overwhelming support and gentle encouragement of my soul mate.

My mentor, friend, and colleague Jane Dunnewold also deserves many thanks. She has not only taught me a great deal about surface design, she has guided me and helped me grow, both professionally and personally. Her gentle and generous spirit has made her a role model for me in work and in life.

The many colleagues, students, and teachers who have come into my life have brought numerous insights and limitless inspiration. Thanks to each and every one of you.

Many thanks to the great team at C&T. From the moment I submitted my book proposal, everyone was exceptionally supportive and helpful. I would particularly like to thank my editor, Lynn Koolish. She guided me through a somewhat daunting task and not only made it seem straightforward but helped make it enjoyable as well.

Contents

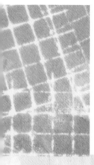

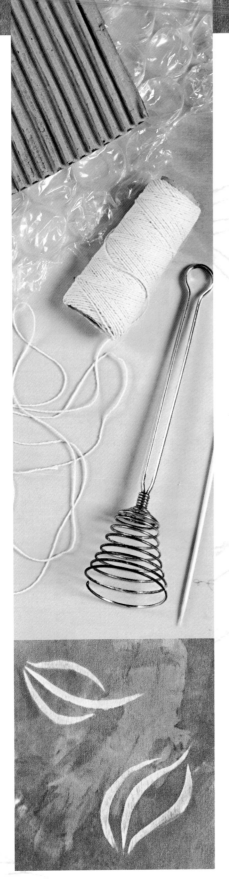

Introduction

Creating a feeling of depth on the flat surface of cloth is challenging and exciting. I am especially fascinated by watching layers of dye and resist build a rich, complex, textured surface. Resist techniques take me back to my childhood, when simple things brought on a sense of wonder and awe. Working with a resist—and seeing the pattern left behind after the resist is washed off—is almost like magic.

A resist is simply a substance that blocks the penetration of dye. Applied directly to fabric before dyeing, it results in an intriguing textured appearance. My fascination with resists began about eight years ago while I was experimenting with a number of paste resists. A few hours with flour paste and potato dextrin and I was hooked! I have since experimented with many organic materials and added a few man-made substances to my repertoire as well.

While exploring the use of resists, I found limited resources on the subject. There were a few books with a chapter on some of the resists, but nothing comprehensive. I have spent many hours experimenting over the past six years to perfect the techniques. My intention for this book is to share what I've learned, to help shorten the learning curve, and to inspire others to experiment with resists.

Using This Book

This book explores the use of eight resists and seven techniques for applying them. Read it from cover to cover or jump right into Applying the Resists (pages 36–59) and start from there. If you have not worked with dyes before, please read Applying Color (pages 60–68) thoroughly—this chapter provides a knowledge base that will be helpful no matter what techniques you choose to work with.

Following are some things to keep in mind while working with resists:

♦ Leave behind any expectations and approach these techniques with a sense of play. Many variables affect the end result, and it may not be what you envisioned. Don't get frustrated—enjoy the serendipity!

♦ Don't give up! If the results of your first effort are disappointing, try a different fabric or application technique, or use a different proportion of water to resist. A small change can make a big difference in the end result.

♦ With the exception of safety guidelines, there are no rules. Pretty much anything goes. So even if I say something doesn't work well, feel free to try it. You may have a different approach that yields success.

Although this book provides a comprehensive guide to working with resists, keep in mind that it is not an exhaustive documentation of all possible techniques. I encourage you to experiment and try different combinations. The possibilities are endless!

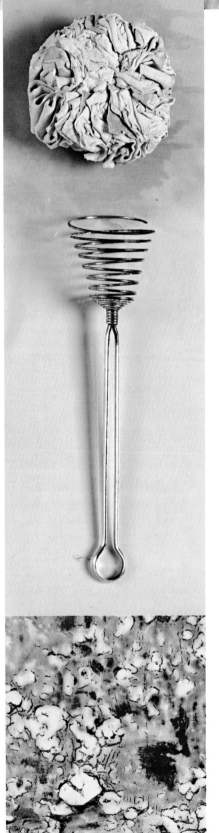

Getting Started

Assembling Your Supplies

Fabric

Use any natural-fiber fabric.

Use any natural-fiber fabric for the techniques in this book. The dyes that are featured work only with natural fibers, so choose from cellulose fibers, such as cotton, linen, rayon, and bamboo, or protein fibers, such as silk or wool. Since the fabric choice will affect the results, it is important to consider the desired outcome and choose an appropriate fabric. For example, many of the resists will not completely penetrate a heavy fabric. This means that there is a greater chance of the dye wicking in from the back. That is not necessarily undesirable; it just means that there will not be a white or almost white area where the resist was. The thickness of the fabric also affects how the dye will react. The dye is more likely to bleed on a very thin fabric, but this can be counteracted by using a thicker dye mixture.

In addition, a fabric with a smooth surface will show more detail and patterning than will a roughly textured fabric, such as silk noil. Silk habotai and rayon are perfect for screen-printing detailed designs with water-based resists. Silk noil and other fabrics with a rough surface are best suited to the crackle and sgraffito effects, as well as less detailed designs.

The fabric choice may also affect the removal of the resist. In general, resists are easier to wash out of lightweight fabrics with a smooth surface. Heavier, textured fabrics, such as silk noil, may require extra scrubbing or washing to remove the resist. Flour and oatmeal, in particular, can be difficult to remove from rougher surfaces.

It is not necessary to purchase "prepared for dyeing" (PFD) fabric. However, it is necessary to remove all sizing before you apply the resist.

Resists

All the resists in this book are easy to obtain, either from a grocery store, from a local craft or art supply store, or over the Internet. A list of suppliers appears in Resources (page 94). More information about the varieties and options is included in The Resists (pages 12–35).

Tools and Equipment

Tools for applying resists

The chapter on applying the resists (pages 36–59) provides a complete materials list for each application method. Depending on the technique used, you may need a squeegee or palette knife, squeeze bottles, syringes, stamps, stencils, silkscreens, and brayers for applying the resists.

It is also helpful to gather a variety of objects to make marks and to scratch into the resists. This is where your creativity comes in. Start looking at everyday objects with an eye for how they can add texture to fabric. Estate sales, thrift shops, hardware stores, discount stores, and even the recycle bin are bountiful with hidden treasures. Following are some suggestions to start your collection:

♦ Anything flat with holes or openings that could be used as a stencil, such as sequin waste, construction fencing, or lace

♦ Items with interesting shapes that could be used as stamps, such as potato mashers, aluminum kitchen scrubbers, and metal hardware items

♦ Textured items that could be placed under the fabric while applying the resist, such as woven place mats, corrugated cardboard, and plastic or metal grids

Once you begin to think about using everyday objects to create patterns on cloth, you will see potential in almost everything!

Gather a variety of containers, measuring cups, and spoons for mixing the resists and dyes. Save plastic containers from the recycle bin. Large yogurt and cottage cheese containers are good for mixing resists. Small yogurt containers are good for mixing dyes.

Start to collect plastic containers for the low water immersion technique. Flat containers are best for this. For small pieces of fabric, a shoebox size works well. For large pieces of fabric, wallpaper trays or under-bed storage boxes are perfect.

Almost anything can be used as a stamp!

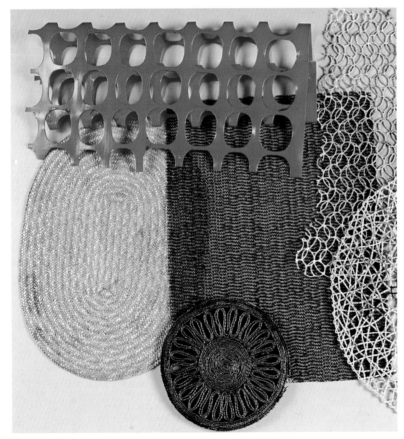

Flat, textured items can be placed under fabric for brayer printing.

Items with holes can be used as stencils.

Plastic containers come in handy for mixing dyes and resists.

If you don't already have a brush collection, start with just a few. Bristle brushes allow greater control and more even application of dye than do foam brushes. Start with a 1" and a 2" flat—both are indispensable for hand painting the dyes. Keep both synthetic- and natural-bristle brushes on hand. The synthetics are great for applying the dyes because of their spring. The bristles bounce back into place after each stroke. Natural-bristle brushes are great for applying resists because the brush strokes will be visible in the final pattern.

A variety of brushes comes in handy for applying resists and dyes.

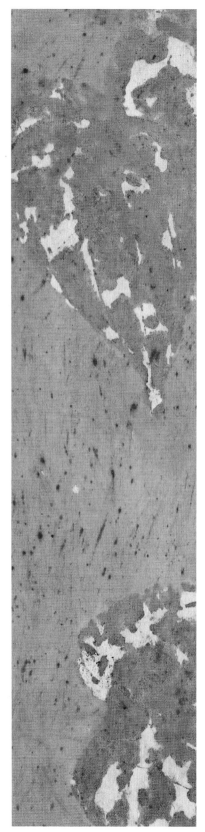

Dyes and Chemicals

MX dyes and auxiliary chemicals

This book focuses on the use of MX fiber-reactive dyes. These dyes are nontoxic, permanent, and easy to use. Soda ash is required to make the dyes permanent, and sodium alginate and urea are required to make thickened dye. Applying Color (pages 60–68) provides complete information on the materials needed for mixing the dyes. Dyes are available at some art supply stores and over the Internet (see Resources, page 94).

Work Surface Preparation

It is helpful to have a dedicated worktable to use these techniques, but it is not necessary. The primary concern is to create the proper surface for the application techniques and to protect the table surface.

A slightly padded work surface works well for most techniques. Use two layers of felt or cotton batting, wrapped and stapled to the bottom of a piece of plywood. The plywood can then be clamped onto a folding table. Use risers to bring the table to the proper height. If your table is doing double duty, try insulation board instead of plywood. It can easily be removed from the table and stored until needed.

Use heavy plastic to protect the work surface from the moisture of the resists. A heavyweight vinyl, available in upholstery departments at fabric stores, works better than plastic drop cloths. Drop cloths can be large and unwieldy, and they need to be folded when not in use. Those folds can create problems by leaving marks on the fabric when you apply the resist or the dye. The heavyweight vinyl has a smooth surface and comes in several thicknesses. It is easier to clean than a plastic drop cloth and can be rolled up for storage.

Heavy vinyl over two layers of felt makes ideal work surface.

When hand painting with dye, place an old sheet on top of the plastic. This will absorb the dye that penetrates the fabric, preventing it from coming through the back of the fabric. Additional sheets come in handy to cover the fabric while the dyes set.

Fabric Preparation

Whether you are using PFD fabric or not, it is imperative that you prewash the fabric before using the resist techniques. Any sizing or finish on the fabric can bond to certain resists, making them difficult or impossible to remove. Even some PFD fabrics have a light starch finish that must be removed. Wash the fabric in hot water with Synthrapol and soda ash. Use a half-teaspoon of each per pound of fabric.

> ### *Tip*
> *Do not use a commercial detergent to prewash the fabric unless you are sure it has no brighteners or fragrances. Also avoid fabric softeners and dryer sheets. These products may contain substances that can impact the dye's ability to bond with the fabric.*

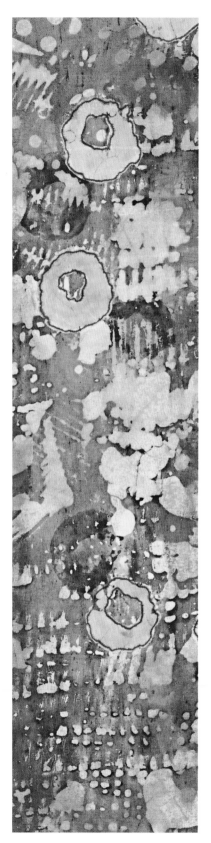

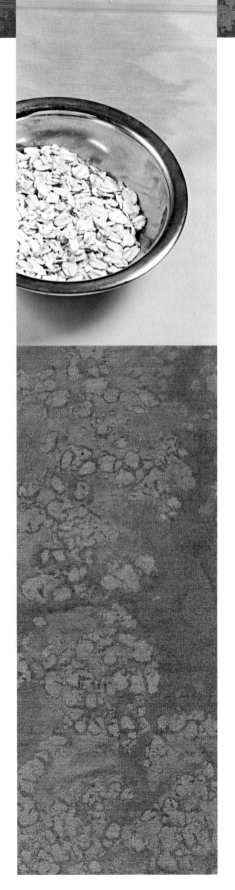

The Resists

Flour

Flour paste is an inexpensive resist that produces stunning crackle effects, and the ingredients are as close as your pantry. This versatile resist is easy to make and easily washes out of the fabric. All-purpose flour works best; however, whole wheat and rice flour can be used for some techniques. Many different types of flour are now available, and many of them can be used to create a paste resist. Because of the variation in gluten content and in texture, each type of flour will produce a slightly different end result. Experiment with these techniques to find your own personal favorites.

Experiment with different varieties of flour.

Materials

- ◆ Flour
- ◆ Water
- ◆ Measuring cup
- ◆ Bowl

- ◆ Wire whisk
- ◆ Tools to apply resist to fabric*

Optional:
- ◆ Handheld blender

* Tools vary depending on the application technique; see pages 36–59.

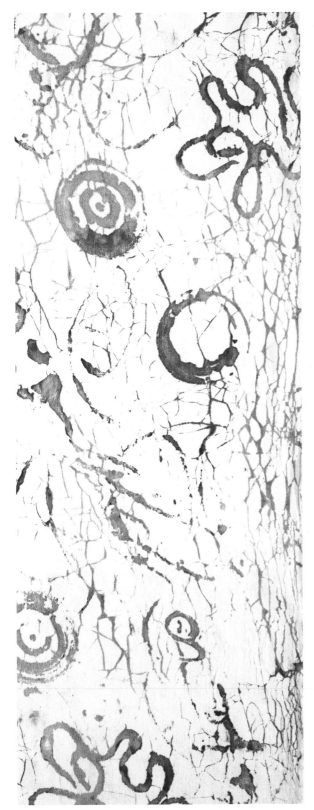

Flour paste applied using sgraffito technique (page 39)

Mixing the Flour Paste

Refer to Applying the Resists (pages 36–59) as needed.

The proper consistency for flour paste depends on how it will be applied and the desired effect. A thicker paste works better for stamping, stenciling, and sgraffito techniques. A thinner paste is easier to spread onto fabric for the crackle effect or to use in a squeeze bottle. The type of flour used and the humidity of the work environment will impact the final consistency of the paste. The recipe below is a starting point. Don't hesitate to adjust the quantity of flour as needed to achieve the desired results.

RECIPE

◆ 1 cup cool water
◆ 1 cup flour

Gradually add the water to the flour, stirring continuously with a wire whisk or handheld blender.

Stir well with wire whisk or handheld blender.

Lumps or No Lumps? It is a matter of personal preference whether to leave in the lumps or remove them. For the crackle effect, leave the lumps in for added texture. For stamping, stenciling, or squeeze-bottle techniques, it is easier to work with smooth, lump-free flour paste. To help eliminate lumps, use a handheld blender to mix the paste.

Tip

Flour paste does not keep well, so make up only the amount needed for your current project.

Applying the Flour Paste to Your Fabric

Refer to Applying the Resists (pages 36–59) as needed.

Flour paste is typically used for the crackle and sgraffito techniques. It can also be used for all the other application techniques except screen printing. The paste will not go through a silkscreen or Thermofax.

If flour is so versatile, why would you choose anything else? One reason is that it doesn't hold up as well to immersion dyeing as some of the other resists. Another reason is that it will crackle no matter how it is applied. If you are using a stencil or stamp and you want a solid image without cracks, try one of the smooth resists, such as corn dextrin (page 23), acrylic medium (page 31), or commercial water-based resists (page 33).

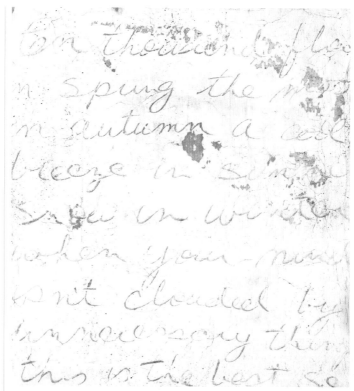

Flour paste applied with squeegee and then scratched into with bamboo skewer

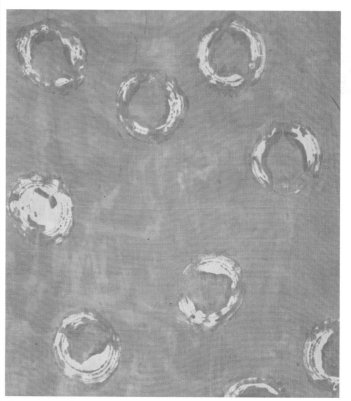

Flour paste applied with spring whisk

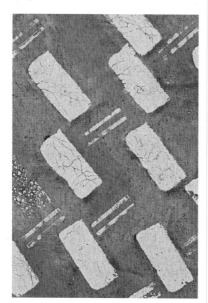

Flour paste applied with sponge stamp and chip clip

Adding Color

Refer to Applying Color (pages 60–68) as needed.

After applying the flour paste, allow it to dry before adding color. The drying time varies, depending on the thickness of the application, the type of fabric, the air temperature, and the humidity of the working environment. It can take from two hours to overnight for the flour to dry completely. To speed up the drying time, set up a fan to blow across the surface of the cloth or hang it on a clothesline after the flour has partially dried. A blow dryer is not recommended, as the heat can make the flour more difficult to remove.

Flour paste works better with hand painting than with immersion. The paste does not penetrate the fabric; rather, it sits on top. In an immersion dye bath, the dye will penetrate the fabric from the back and the paste will begin to break down. This reduces its resist properties. However, immersion can produce interesting, subtle effects. Prepare a thicker version of the paste mixture to help it withstand the immersion.

Flour paste applied with a squeegee and then stamped with corrugated cardboard and immersed

Flour paste applied to scrunched fabric

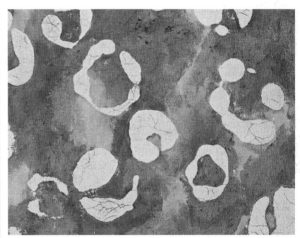

Flour paste applied with squeeze bottle

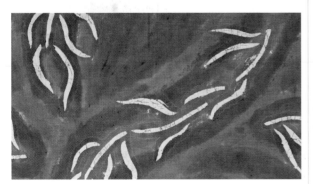

Flour paste applied through stencil

Flour paste applied with bristle brush

Photo by Lynn Luukinen

Oatmeal

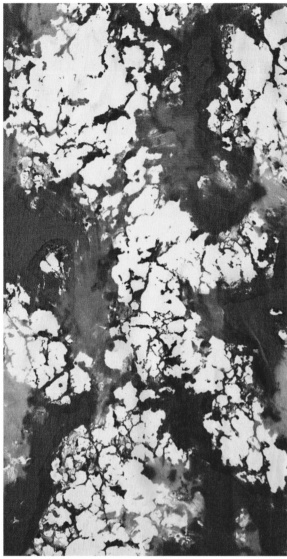

Oatmeal prepared with hot water method

Oatmeal is another readily available, inexpensive resist, and it produces a very distinct crackle effect. It is less versatile than other resists and takes more effort to remove, but it produces a beautiful pattern that can't be achieved any other way. It is easy to make and will yield a variety of results depending on how you prepare it. Avoid using quick or instant oatmeal. The grains are finely chopped and don't produce the same patterning effect as whole or rolled oats.

Materials

- ◆ Oats
- ◆ Water
- ◆ Measuring cup
- ◆ Bowl
- ◆ Spoon
- ◆ Wooden spoon or squeegee to apply resist to fabric*

Optional:
- ◆ Microwave oven and microwave-safe container

* Tools vary depending on the application technique; see pages 36–59.

Use whole rather than quick-cooking oats.

Mixing the Oatmeal

The oatmeal must be cooked or prepared with hot water. Otherwise, it will simply crack and fall off the fabric when dry. A variety of patterning effects can be achieved by altering how long the oatmeal is cooked and the ratio of water to oats. A longer cooking time and a higher ratio of water to oats will yield a soft marbled effect. Less water and a shorter cooking time yield a distinctive oat-grain pattern. The recipes below are a starting point. Adjust the quantity of oats and cooking times as needed to achieve the desired results.

> ## Tip
> *The oatmeal will not keep well, so mix up only the amount needed for your current project.*

Oatmeal ready to be applied to fabric

MICROWAVE METHOD

- ⅓ cup oats
- 1 cup water

Add the water to the oats in a microwave-safe container. Microwave for 1–2 minutes. Allow the mixture to sit 5–7 minutes before using. Apply warm or cool.

HOT WATER METHOD

- 1 cup oats
- 1 cup boiling water

Add the oatmeal to the boiling water. Stir the mixture and let it sit for 5–10 minutes. This will produce a very distinct oat-grain patterning. For a more marbled look, use less oatmeal. The mixture can be applied warm or cold.

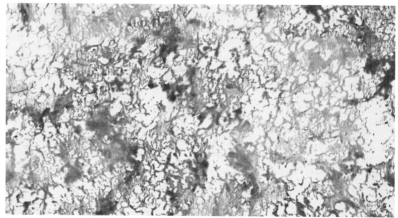

Microwaved oats yield softer, less detailed pattern.

Use hot water method to retain distinctive oat pattern.

Applying the Oatmeal to Your Fabric

Oatmeal works best with the crackle technique (page 36). Its thickness and texture make it difficult to use with other application techniques.

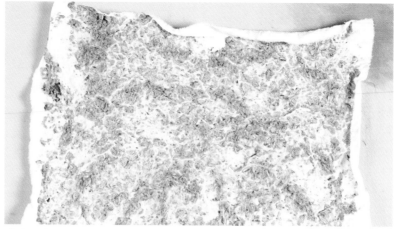

Cloth with dried oatmeal resist ready for hand painting or immersion

Adding Color

Refer to Applying Color (pages 60–68) as needed.

After applying the oatmeal to the fabric, allow it to dry before adding color. The drying time varies, depending on the thickness of the application, the type of fabric, the air temperature, and the humidity of the working environment. It can take one to three days for the oatmeal to dry completely. To speed up the drying time, set up a fan to blow across the surface of the cloth or hang the fabric on a clothesline once the oats have partially dried.

Oatmeal works well with hand painting and immersion. A more distinct pattern is visible when the fabric is hand painted. When the cloth is immersed, the dye will penetrate the fabric from the back, resulting in a softer, mottled appearance.

Hot water method, low water immersion

Cooked method, low water immersion

Sugar

Sugar syrup with wet-on-wet technique

Sugar is inexpensive, easy to obtain, and perfect for wet-on-wet (page 65) techniques. When cooked, sugar thickens and forms a syrup. This syrup is very smooth and works well for squeeze-bottle applications. It is a cost-effective alternative to commercial resists; however, it will dissolve more easily, leaving a soft edge. The main drawback to sugar syrup is that it can be very sticky.

Materials

- ♦ Confectioner's sugar
- ♦ Water
- ♦ Measuring cup
- ♦ Bowl
- ♦ Spoon or wire whisk
- ♦ Hot plate or stovetop burner
- ♦ Small saucepan
- ♦ Tools to apply resist to fabric*

Tools vary depending on the application technique; see pages 36–59.

Use confectioner's sugar to make syrup.

Mixing the Sugar Syrup

RECIPE

- ◆ 1 cup confectioner's sugar
- ◆ 1 cup water

Place the sugar in a small saucepan. Add the water and stir. Bring the mixture to a simmer and cook uncovered for 15–20 minutes or until thickened. Stir frequently. The syrup should be the consistency of heavy cream and the volume will be reduced by ⅓ to ½. Let the mixture cool. The syrup will keep in the refrigerator for several weeks. If the syrup has thickened, place it in a microwave oven for 10–20 seconds to soften.

Thickened sugar syrup, ready for application

Applying the Sugar Syrup to Your Fabric

Refer to Applying the Resists (pages 36–59) as needed.

Because sugar syrup is very smooth, it is perfect for squeeze-bottle, stamping, and stenciling applications. It is also one of the best resists to use for the wet-on-wet technique. Its sticky nature makes it difficult to use for brayer printing and screen printing, and it is not appropriate for crackle or sgraffito techniques.

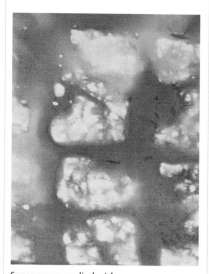

Sugar syrup applied with sponge stamp, painted while wet

Adding Color

Refer to Applying Color (pages 60–68) as needed.

After applying the sugar mixture, allow it to dry before adding color. The drying time varies, depending on the thickness of the application, the type of fabric, the air temperature, and the humidity of the working environment. It can take from several hours to overnight for the syrup to dry completely. To speed up the drying time, set up a fan to blow across the surface of the cloth. A blow dryer is not recommended, as the heat can melt the syrup. Do not hang the cloth to dry, unless you want the resulting drips that will occur.

Color can be applied by hand painting or immersion. Sugar is water soluble, but a thick application of the resist can withstand low water immersion. The dye will breach the resist, leaving a soft ghostlike image.

Sugar syrup applied with squeeze bottle and then hand painted

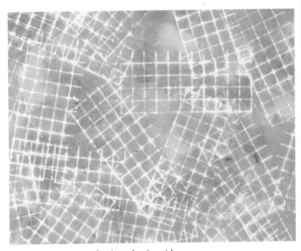

Sugar syrup applied with squeeze bottle and then immersed

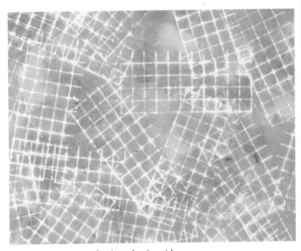

Sugar syrup stamped using plastic grid

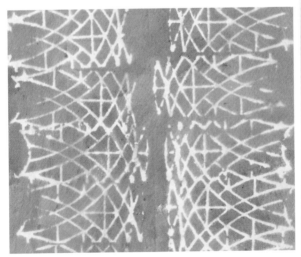

Sugar syrup applied with brayer-printing technique

Potato Dextrin

Potato dextrin with crackle technique

Potato dextrin is very easy to work with, and it can be used in a variety of techniques. Once mixed, it will keep in the refrigerator for several weeks. This resist comes in the form of a fine white powder derived from potatoes. It mixes into a smooth paste that cracks as it dries. These cracks create a very distinctive patterning on the cloth, quite different from that obtained with flour paste (page 12). Potato dextrin is available from surface design suppliers (see Resources, page 94).

Materials

- Potato dextrin
- Water
- Measuring cup
- Bowl
- Wire whisk or handheld blender
- Tools to apply resist to fabric*

Tools vary depending on the application technique; see pages 36–59.

Potato dextrin is smooth white powder available from surface design suppliers.

Mixing the Potato Dextrin

RECIPE

- 1¼ cups potato dextrin
- 1 cup boiling water

Slowly add the dextrin to the water while stirring with a wire whisk or handheld blender. Stir until the dextrin is completely blended and smooth. Let the mixture sit 10–15 minutes to thicken and cool slightly. It should be the consistency of heavy cream. If there is a frothy layer on top of the dextrin, remove it with a spoon.

Slowly add dextrin to water, stirring continuously.

The manufacturer's directions recommend using the dextrin when it is about 85°F. I prefer to let it cool to room temperature. This produces a thicker mixture that is easier to work with and that creates a larger crackle pattern.

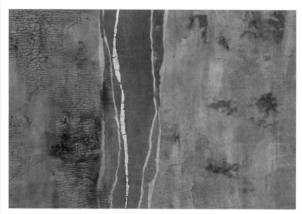

Pattern created with day-old dextrin (*left*); pattern created with fresh dextrin (*right*)

Leftover paste will keep in the refrigerator for 3–4 weeks. To use, allow the paste to come to room temperature or microwave for 30 seconds, and then stir until smooth.

Tip

For any of the application techniques other than the crackle, a slightly thicker version works better. Achieve this by adding a little more dextrin or letting the dextrin sit overnight.

Applying the Potato Dextrin to Your Fabric

Potato dextrin is extremely versatile and can be used in a variety of ways. The basic approach is to spread it over the entire surface of the cloth to create its signature crackle pattern; however, it can also be applied with an assortment of tools. All the techniques for applying resists (pages 36–59) are appropriate for use with potato dextrin.

Potato dextrin applied with brayer

Potato dextrin sgraffito created with circular brush

Potato dextrin applied through plastic grid

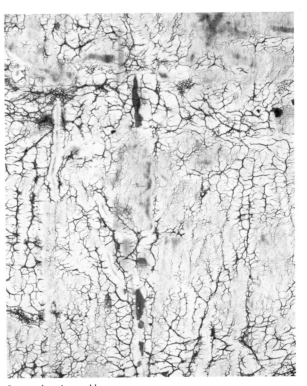

Potato dextrin crackle

Adding Color

Refer to Applying Color (pages 60–68) as needed.

After applying the dextrin, allow it to dry before adding color. The drying time varies, depending on the thickness of the application, the type of fabric, the air temperature, and the humidity of the working environment. It can take from two hours to overnight for the dextrin to dry completely. To speed up the drying time, set up a fan to blow across the surface of the cloth. A blow dryer is not recommended, as the heat can melt the dextrin.

The crackle pattern cannot be achieved through immersion, so hand painting is required for that application technique. The colors are often more washed out when using the dextrin for the crackle effect, so mix the dyes a bit darker than normal.

If the dextrin is stamped on with a sponge or applied with a stencil, it usually creates a thick enough coating to withstand low water immersion. The dextrin is water soluble, so immersion creates a softer effect, as the dextrin dissolves slightly.

Potato dextrin applied with sponge stamp and hand painted

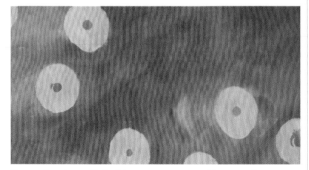

Potato dextrin applied with sponge stamp and immersed

Corn Dextrin

Corn dextrin applied with stencil

Corn dextrin is specially formulated to mix into a smooth paste. This property makes it perfect for squeeze-bottle and stenciling applications. Corn dextrin comes in the form of a fine white powder, which looks very much like potato dextrin. It creates a very different effect, however. It does not crack as it dries, so it produces patterns with a smooth appearance. Corn dextrin is available from surface design suppliers (see Resources, page 94).

Materials

♦ Corn dextrin
♦ Water
♦ Measuring cup
♦ Bowl
♦ Wire whisk or handheld blender
♦ Tools to apply resist to fabric*

Tools vary depending on the application technique; see pages 36–59.

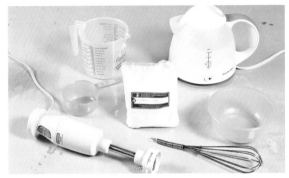

Corn dextrin looks similar to potato dextrin but produces different results.

Mixing the Corn Dextrin

RECIPE

♦ 1¼ cups corn dextrin
♦ 1 cup boiling water

Slowly add the dextrin to the water while stirring with a wire whisk or handheld blender. Stir until the dextrin is completely blended and smooth. Let the mixture sit 10–15 minutes to thicken. The mixture can be applied warm or cool. Leftover paste will keep in the refrigerator for 3–4 weeks. To use, allow the paste to come to room temperature or microwave it for 30–60 seconds, and then stir until smooth.

Slowly add dextrin to water, stirring continuously.

Applying the Corn Dextrin to Your Fabric

Refer to Applying the Resists (pages 36–59) as needed.

Corn dextrin is extremely versatile and can be applied in a variety of ways. It is appropriate for squeeze-bottle, stamping, stenciling, screen-printing, and brayer-printing applications. It does not crack, so it is not appropriate for the crackle technique. It also does not work well for the sgraffito technique.

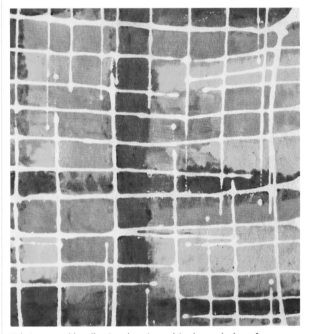

Fabric created by allowing dextrin to drip down cloth surface

Fabric with dextrin stamped with window chamois

Adding Color

Refer to Applying Color (pages 60–68) as needed.

After applying the corn dextrin, allow it to dry before adding color. The drying time varies, depending on the thickness of the application, the type of fabric, the air temperature, and the humidity of the working environment. It can take from two hours to overnight for the dextrin to dry completely. To speed up the drying time, set up a fan to blow across the surface of the cloth. A blow dryer is not recommended, as the heat can melt the dextrin.

Corn dextrin creates a fairly strong resist, so it can withstand immersion. Keep in mind that the dextrin is water soluble, so immersion yields a design with softer edges than if the fabric is hand painted.

Corn dextrin brushed through drain plate and hand painted

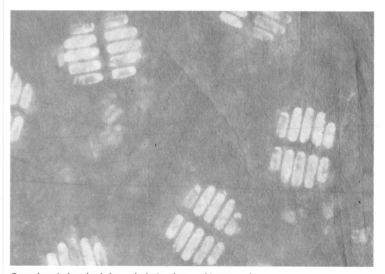

Corn dextrin brushed through drain plate and immersed

Dextrin brushed through lacy fabric

Soy Wax

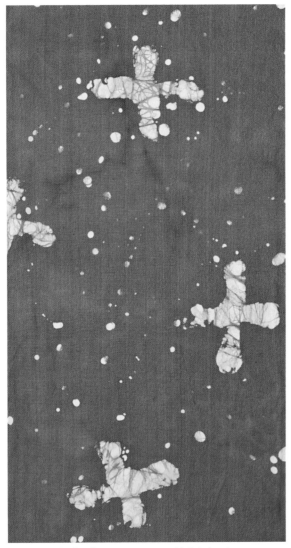

Soy wax applied with sponge stamp and bristle brush

Soy wax is a relatively new product, made from hydrogenated soybean oil. One of the primary benefits of soy wax is that it melts at a fairly low temperature. This allows it to be removed by washing in hot water, which is much easier than the ironing or dry cleaning required of paraffin or beeswax. Another benefit is that it does not give off toxic fumes, so ventilation is less of a concern than with paraffin. Soy wax has been a boon to surface designers who like the look of batik but do not want the inconvenience of working with paraffin or beeswax.

Soy wax is available from a number of suppliers that focus on surface design applications, as well as those that specialize in candle making. Although soy wax is available from a variety of sources, purchase wax designed for textile use because it is a high-quality wax that easily washes out. Some of the candle blends have additional ingredients that make them difficult, if not impossible, to remove. Refer to Resources (page 94) for sources of good-quality soy wax.

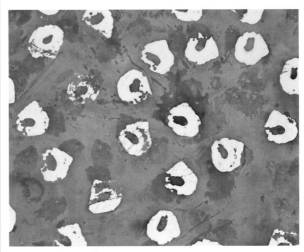

Soy wax applied with sponge stamp

Materials

- ◆ Soy wax flakes
- ◆ Electric skillet, dedicated to wax use
- ◆ Wax thermometer
- ◆ Tools to apply resist to fabric*

Tools vary depending on the application technique; see pages 36–59.

Soy wax comes in easy-to-use flakes.

Melting the Wax

Soy wax comes in flakes and melts at approximately 140°F. The flakes melt quickly and are easy to use. Soy wax is flammable, so it is important to follow safety guidelines (at right). Use a candle thermometer to maintain a safe temperature.

Although there are several methods for melting soy wax, an electric skillet is ideal. Most electric skillets have a thermostat, which allows more precise temperature control than other melting methods. To melt the wax, pour the flakes into a skillet. Set the thermostat to 180°–200°F. If the wax is bubbling or smoking, set it to a lower temperature. When you are finished using the wax, let it cool in the skillet. The wax can be melted again and used later.

Tip

Keep in mind that each appliance may be slightly different. Use a candle thermometer to check the temperature of the wax in your appliance.

Melt soy wax in electric skillet.

Soy Wax Safety Guidelines

◆ Soy wax is flammable, so never melt it over an open flame.

◆ Do not leave hot soy wax unattended.

◆ Although soy wax is nontoxic, when heated to a high temperature it emits an oil mist that can be harmful to the respiratory system. Use the lowest temperature setting that will keep the wax melted. If the wax is bubbling or smoking, set the skillet to a lower temperature.

◆ Clip a candle thermometer to the melting pot to ensure that the temperature does not get too hot.

◆ Use caution when working with melted soy wax; it can burn if it touches exposed skin.

◆ Read the Material Safety Data Sheet for complete safety information. This is available from the supplier.

Applying the Soy Wax to Your Fabric

Refer to Applying the Resists (pages 36–59) as needed.

Tools used to apply soy wax

Soy wax works well with direct application techniques. It can be applied with almost any tool, including stencils, brushes, tjantings, or sponges. You can also dip fabric directly into the wax. The wax cools relatively quickly, so it is not appropriate for applying with a squeeze bottle or a silkscreen. Instead, use a tjanting to create detailed designs with soy wax.

Using a tjanting takes a little bit of practice, but once mastered it is a versatile tool. Draw, write, or create fine lines and dots with it. Tjangings have a reservoir to hold the wax and a tip from which the wax drips out. They come in various sizes, so choose the opening size best suited to your design. Applying the Resists (pages 36–59) provides step-by-step instructions on additional methods of applying wax to fabric.

Fill reservoir of tjanting with hot wax.

Tip tjanting slightly backward to prevent wax from coming out of tip.

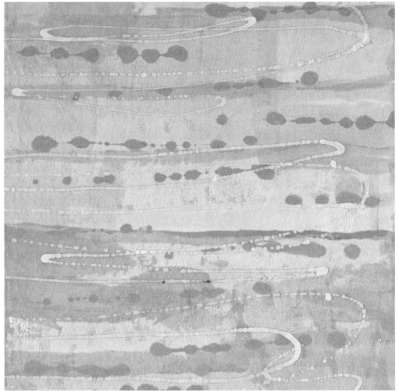

Wax applied with tjanting; fabric then hand painted with thickened dye

Tip

Hold a small piece of paper or cloth under the tip of the tjanting while moving it from the wax pot to the cloth to prevent unwanted drips.

Tip tjanting forward so wax can drip out of tip; it works well for text and drawing.

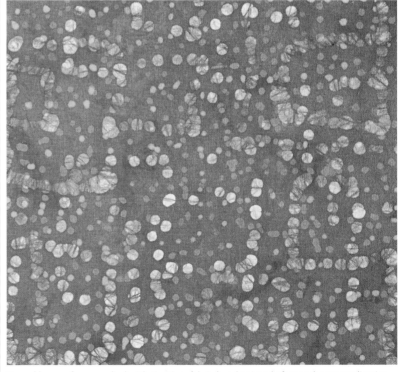

Several layers of wax applied with tjanting; fabric hand painted after each wax application

Tip

Let the tjanting sit in the melted wax for at least 10 minutes to warm up the metal reservoir. This keeps the wax in the tjanting melted for a longer period of time.

Soy wax applied with brush

Soy wax applied with variety of found objects

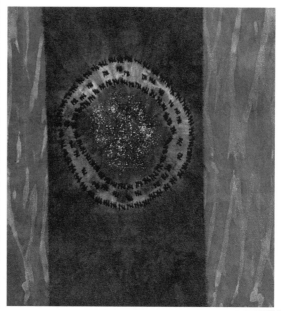

Soy wax applied to fabric wrapped on PVC pipe (detail of *This Moment*, page 86)

Tip

When you are applying the wax, it should appear clear and go through to the back side of the fabric. If it looks opaque and doesn't penetrate the fabric, it is not hot enough.

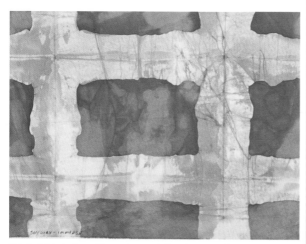

Fabric folded, dipped into wax, and then immersed

Cleanup

Although soy wax can be washed out of the tools with hot water, it is difficult to remove all the wax, especially from sponges and bristle brushes. It also takes a lot of water, so I prefer to keep a dedicated set of tools to use with wax. The wax hardens on the tool, and it quickly melts when placed in hot wax.

Excess wax can be scraped off your vinyl work surface (page 10) and placed back into the melting pot for reuse. A solvent-based cleaner, such as Goo Gone or Citra Solv, will remove any wax residue from the vinyl work surface.

Scrape excess wax off work surface and place it in wax pot to reuse.

Adding Color

Refer to Applying Color (pages 60–68) as needed.

One of the benefits of working with soy wax is that you can apply color within five to ten minutes of applying the wax. As long as the wax has cooled, the fabric can be painted.

Soy wax lends itself to both immersion dyeing and hand painting. The combination of water and soda ash does tend to break down the wax, particularly in immersion dyeing. Therefore, the quality of the line is softer with an immersion dye than with hand painting.

Soy wax brushed on; fabric then hand painted with thickened dye

Soy wax brushed on; fabric then placed in low water dye immersion

Tips

Immersion Dyeing with Soy Wax

Place the fabric in the refrigerator or freezer after the wax has been applied. This helps the wax withstand the immersion better. Be sure to wrap the fabric in a bag to prevent wax pieces from chipping off into the refrigerator or freezer. After mixing the dye, allow it to cool slightly—keeping the dye at the low range of the recommended temperature for MX dyes (75°–85°F) will help prevent the wax from melting.

Soy wax stamped with carved sponge; fabric then immersed

Acrylic Medium

Acrylic medium applied with Thermofax screen

Acrylic medium is a water-based emulsion typically used to modify acrylic paints. It comes in a variety of forms, both liquid and gel. It is creamy white and dries clear. Water soluble while wet, it becomes permanent on the fabric when dry. It does affect the hand of the fabric, particularly lightweight silks. Textile medium is a similar product that is designed to be used on textiles and leaves less stiffness on the fabric. Either product is suitable as a resist. Acrylic medium is used straight from the bottle.

Acrylic or textile medium is available at art supply stores and most craft and hobby stores. Two common brands of acrylic medium are Liquitex and Golden. Some art supply stores also carry their own brands.

When applied in a very thin coating, acrylic medium sometimes has the opposite effect of what is expected. It wicks in the color and makes the fabric darker rather than leaving white or lighter areas. This property can be used intentionally to good effect. Try applying thicker coatings in some areas and thinner coatings in other areas.

Acrylic medium is available in a variety of formulations—liquid or gel and matte or gloss finish. Any of them can be used as a resist, but the liquid mediums leave a softer hand. The final effect will depend on the variety used, so experiment to see which you prefer.

Acrylic mediums can be used as resists.

Materials

- Acrylic or textile medium
- Tools to apply resist to fabric*

Tools vary depending on the application technique; see pages 36–59.

Applying Acrylic Medium to Your Fabric

Acrylic medium is best suited to stenciling (page 45), stamping (page 48), screen-printing (page 52), and brayer-printing (page 56) applications. It quickly soaks into the fabric and is not suitable for crackle (page 36) or sgraffito (page 39) techniques. Although it is suitable for squeeze-bottle techniques (page 42), be sure to use a fine tip, or it will create a permanent three-dimensional line on the fabric surface.

Because of its tendency to affect the hand of the fabric, it is best used in small quantities and with techniques that do not leave a heavy coating on the fabric. If you plan to immerse the cloth rather than hand paint it, the medium will resist better if it penetrates the fabric.

Leaf print with textile medium

> ### Tip
>
> *Do not let acrylic medium dry on your tools. It will not wash out after it has dried!*

Fabric stenciled with liquid matte medium

Acrylic medium applied with syringe

Adding Color

Refer to Applying Color (pages 60–68) as needed.

Acrylic medium lends itself to both immersion dyeing and hand painting. It dries quickly, so the fabric can be immersed or hand painted within an hour or two.

> ### Tip
> *Iron the fabric before applying the dye. This gives the medium greater resist properties and softens the hand of the fabric.*

Fabric screen-printed with acrylic medium and then hand painted

Fabric screen-printed with acrylic medium and then immersed

Water-Based Resists

Water-based resist applied with brayer printing

A number of products intended for use as resists are currently on the market. Many of these were designed for silk painting, a technique in which the resist is applied with a squeeze bottle and then liquid dyes are painted inside the lines. These products are extremely versatile as resists. Water-based resists are great for those who have allergies or respiratory problems and can't use discharge agents. These resists can create a look similar to that achieved by discharging. Water-based resists are ready to use—no mixing is required. This helps achieve consistency on large projects or across a series of pieces.

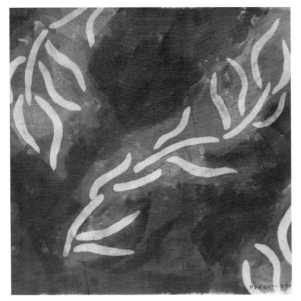

Faux discharge effect with water-based resist

Some examples of water-based resists are Presist, Jacquard Water-Based Resist, and SilkPaint water-based resist.

An economical and readily available alternative is Elmer's Washable School Glue Gel. The downside is that it does not provide as strong of a resist.

The products are all slightly different—some keep a crisper line, some tend to bleed into the fabric more, some wash out more easily than others, and some will hold up better in an immersion dye bath. Experiment to determine which brand works best for the techniques you prefer.

Water-based resists are available at some art supply stores. The many Internet-based surface design suppliers (see Resources, page 94) also offer a wide variety of options.

Commercially available water-based resists

Materials

♦ Water-based resist
♦ Tools to apply resist to fabric*

* Tools vary depending on the application technique; see pages 36–59.

Applying Water-Based Resists to Your Fabric

Water-based resists are very smooth—the consistency of honey. They do not crack when dried and so are not appropriate for the crackle effect (page 36). They do work well with all the other application techniques. They are especially suited to screen-printing applications (page 52) because of their smooth texture.

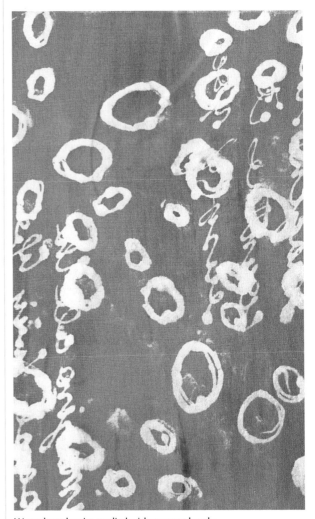

Water-based resist applied with squeeze bottle

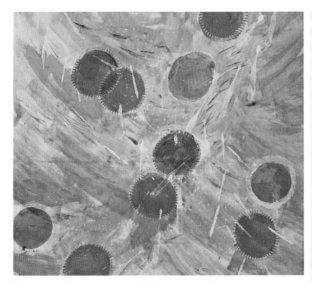

Water-based resist applied with kitchen utensils

Water-based resist applied with palette knife and circular bristle brush

Adding Color

Refer to Applying Color (pages 60–68) as needed.

A water-based resist dries quickly if it is applied in a thin coating, so the fabric can be immersed or hand painted within an hour or two. If you apply a thick coating, it may take a day or more to dry completely.

Water-based resists can be used for hand painting as well as immersion dyeing. However, each brand of water-based resist is different. Some stand up better to immersion than others, so test a sample before you work on a large project.

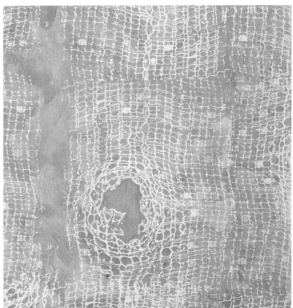

Fabric screen-printed with water-based resist and then hand painted

Fabric screen-printed with water-based resist and then immersed

Applying the Resists

There are unlimited alternatives when it comes to applying the resists to fabric. This chapter presents seven approaches, many of them with several variations. Please don't be limited to these—experiment and create your own techniques!

If you apply a resist and are not happy with the resulting pattern, wash out the resist and start over. (Note that acrylic medium will only wash out if it hasn't dried. The other resists can be washed out even if they are dry.) Some techniques are not appropriate for all resists. A good understanding of the properties of a particular resist will help you determine which techniques work best. The Recommended Application Techniques for Each Resist chart (page 93) indicates the recommended techniques for each resist.

Crackle

Refer to The Resists (pages 12–35) as needed.

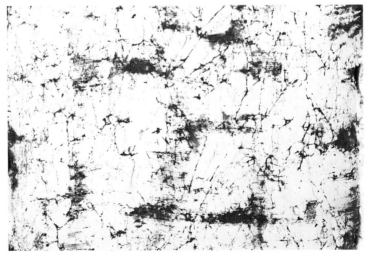

Flour paste applied with crackle technique

The crackle technique is quite straightforward. It is appropriate for those resists that crack as they dry on the fabric. The cracks allow dye to penetrate, creating an interesting texture. Flour paste, oatmeal, and potato dextrin are the best resists to use for this method. Soy wax can be used for this technique, but when applied in large areas it creates a thick coating of wax on the cloth that may be difficult to remove.

Materials

♦ Natural-fiber fabric
♦ Pins
♦ Paste resist of choice
♦ Tool to apply resist (such as squeegee, wooden spoon, palette knife, or spatula)
♦ Bristle brush (1″–3″ flat brush, depending on size of fabric)
♦ MX fiber-reactive dyes

Technique

1. Pin the fabric to the plastic-covered work surface (page 10) or use masking tape to adhere the edges. Place the pins 2″–3″ apart at the top of the fabric and 4″–5″ apart at the sides. The fabric will stretch slightly when dampened by the resist, so pull the fabric taut when pinning or taping.

Tip

Leave the bottom half of the fabric loose. The fabric will stretch when the damp resist is applied, and if pinned the fabric may wrinkle while you are spreading the resist.

2. Prepare the resist (pages 12–35).

3. Pour the resist along an edge of the cloth. Use a squeegee, spoon, or palette knife to spread the paste over the cloth, pouring on more resist as needed. The drying time varies, depending on the thickness of the application, the type of fabric, the air temperature, and the humidity of the working environment. To speed up the drying time, set up a fan to blow across the surface of the cloth. A blow dryer is not recommended, as the heat can make the resist more difficult to remove. Another alternative is to hang the cloth on a clothesline after it has partially dried.

Tips

● *If you are working with oatmeal, use a large wooden spoon or spatula to apply the resist.*

● *If you are using potato dextrin, it will soak into the fabric if the paste is too thin or if it is applied too thinly. This produces a layer too thin to crack when it is dry. If the dextrin has been absorbed into the cloth, apply another layer of dextrin on top of the first.*

Pour resist onto cloth.

Pull resist across fabric with squeegee.

Tip

To achieve a greater crackle effect, roll up the cloth and squeeze it to crack the resist. The more the cloth is squeezed, the more cracking will occur, allowing more dye to penetrate the resist. Shake the loose bits of resist into the trash can before painting the fabric with dye.

4. After the resist has dried, follow the directions for applying color and washing out the fabric in Applying Color (pages 60–68).

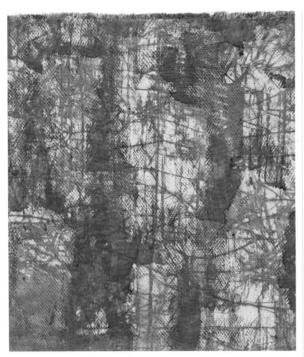

Soy wax with crackle effect

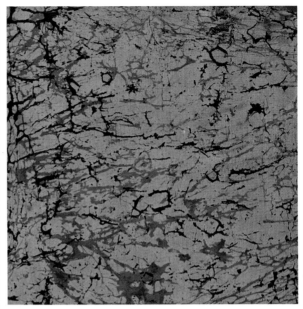

Fabric coated with two layers of flour paste crackle and then overdyed

Tip

Unpin a corner and look at the back of the cloth to get a sneak preview of the patterning and to see how much dye is penetrating the resist. If more patterning is desired, brush more dye into the cracks or add a small amount of water to thin the dye slightly. Keep in mind that with heavy fabrics, the amount of crackling on the front will be greater than what appears on the back.

Back of cloth with oatmeal resist

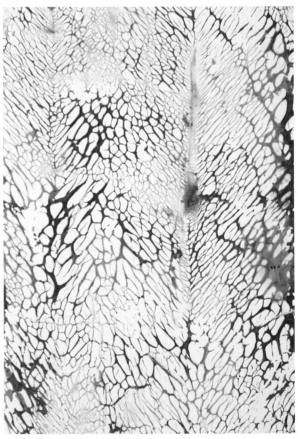

Potato dextrin applied unevenly, leaving some areas with large crackle pattern and others with fine crackle pattern

Oatmeal crackle pattern

Crackle Variations

Rather than applying flour paste or potato dextrin with a squeegee, try a 2″ natural-bristle brush. The brush strokes will create marks that show on the final cloth. This is a great way to create a sense of movement on the cloth.

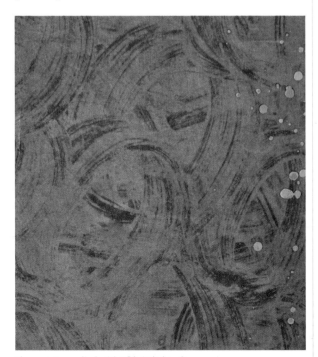

Flour paste applied with 2″ bristle brush

Sgraffito

Refer to The Resists (pages 12–35) as needed.

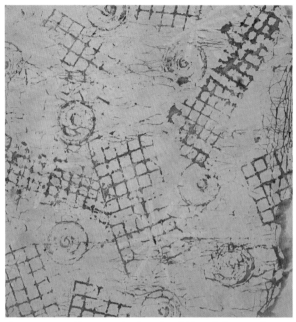

Flour paste sgraffito created using wire whisk and plastic grid

The word "sgraffito" comes from an Italian word meaning "to scratch." As an art technique, it means to scratch into the surface to reveal what is below. Sgraffito was traditionally used on plaster walls or ceramics and is now commonly used in oil or acrylic paintings to create depth and texture.

Applied to resist techniques, sgraffito involves scratching into the surface of a moist resist with a variety of objects to create a pattern. This technique is perfect for creating text or drawing a design. A variation on this is to place textured items such as bubble wrap, hardware cloth, or other such materials on freshly applied resist and then remove them before the resist dries completely. This creates interesting patterns that appear after the fabric is painted with dye.

The sgraffito technique works best with flour paste and potato dextrin. It can be used with sugar syrup and commercial resists if they are thick enough, but it produces a less distinct pattern because the resist tends to be absorbed into the fabric. Sgraffito can also be used with soy wax; however, this will leave a heavy coating of wax on the fabric that can be difficult to remove.

Materials

♦ Natural-fiber fabric
♦ Pins
♦ Resist of choice
♦ Tool to apply resist (such as squeegee, wooden spoon, palette knife, or spatula)
♦ Bristle brush (1"–3" flat brush, depending on size of fabric)
♦ Tools for scratching into surface of cloth (such as bamboo skewer, notched spreader, or kitchen utensils)
♦ Textured items to place on the moist resist (such as corrugated cardboard, lace, woven place mats, or rubber bands)
♦ MX fiber-reactive dyes

Collect objects to add texture with sgraffito.

Technique

1. Follow Steps 1–3 for the crackle technique (page 36).

2. While the resist is still moist, scratch into the surface with a bamboo skewer, notched spreader, or other tool.

Use bamboo skewer to write or draw into resist.

Flour paste scratched into with bamboo skewer

Tips

For flour or potato dextrin (pages 12 and 20): Use slightly less water when mixing the resist. A thicker version will hold up better. If the resist seeps back into the marks, let the resist dry for 10–15 minutes and try again.

For soy wax (page 26): Wait until the wax has cooled before scratching into the surface.

3. After the resist has dried, follow the directions for applying color and washing out the fabric in Applying Color (pages 60–68).

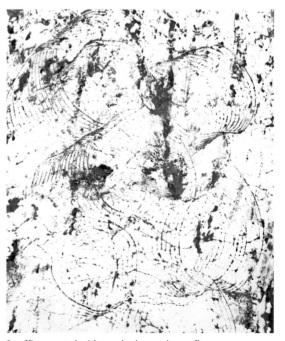
Sgraffito created with notched spreader on flour paste

Sgraffito Variation

An alternative to scratching into the surface is to press items with pattern and texture into the moist resist. Woven place mats or trivets, rug grippers, and net produce bags are all excellent candidates for this technique. For a different look, place rubber bands, paper clips, and other small objects on top of the moist resist. Press down lightly on each object. If the resist is thick enough, remove the object immediately; if the resist seeps back into the marks, lay the object back in place and leave it for 5–20 minutes. This variation does not work well with soy wax because it cools so quickly.

> ### Tip
> *Be sure to remove the items while the resist is still moist. Otherwise, you may pull up large areas of resist when removing the objects.*

Place textured items on fabric while resist is moist.

Remove items before resist has dried.

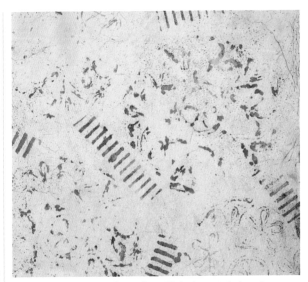

Trivet left faint image and cardboard left clear vertical marks.

Sgraffito with potato dextrin

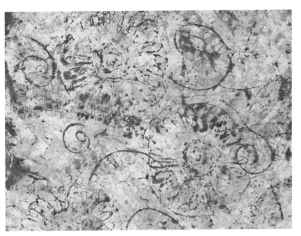

Sgraffito with flour paste

Squeeze Bottle

Refer to The Resists (pages 12–35) as needed.

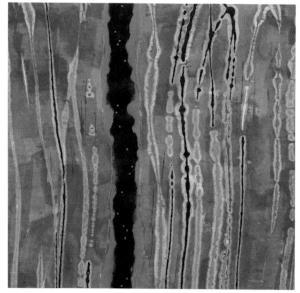

Sugar syrup applied with squeeze bottle (detail of *Flow,* page 87)

A squeeze bottle is great for writing, drawing, or creating free-form designs. It can be used with a spontaneous, intuitive approach or it can be used to create a preplanned pattern. Variations on this technique include dripping the resist from the end of a spoon and extruding the resist from a syringe. This technique is appropriate for all the resists except oatmeal and soy wax. The wax cools too quickly to use in a bottle; however, the use of a tjanting provides the same effect (page 27).

Materials

♦ Natural-fiber fabric
♦ Pins
♦ Resist of choice
♦ Squeeze bottle, syringe, or spoon
♦ Bristle brush (1"–3" flat brush, depending on size of fabric)
♦ MX fiber-reactive dyes

Optional:
♦ Items to drag through resist (such as notched spreader, brush, or palette knife)
♦ Fabric marking pen
♦ Wooden frame for stretching fabric

Technique

1. Pin the fabric to the work surface at 8"–10" intervals or use masking tape to adhere the edges.

2. Prepare the resist (pages 12–35). It is very important to remove all the lumps for this technique. Put the resist through a mesh strainer, if necessary, and then pour the resist into a squeeze bottle. This can be a bit messy and tedious. Have patience and use a funnel—the results are worth it!

Tip

Keep a variety of squeeze bottles on hand. Raid your recycle bin for mustard and ketchup bottles. Collect bottles with a variety of tips. Craft stores sell a variety of metal tips for plastic squeeze bottles. The tip size to use is determined by the resist, the fabric, and the desired design. A lightweight silk generally requires a finer tip than is needed for a heavier fabric. Paste resists need a larger tip than commercial water-based resists. A detailed design is easier to obtain with a finer-tipped bottle.

Start collection of squeeze bottles.

3. Squeeze the resist onto the fabric, either randomly or in a predrawn design. Allow the resist to dry.

Squeeze resist onto fabric.

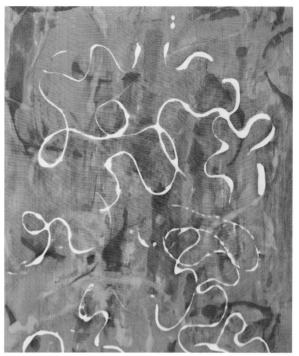

Potato dextrin applied with syringe

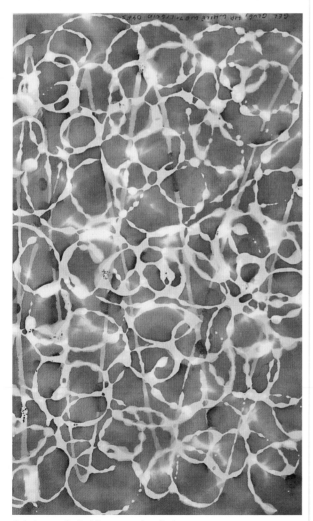

Gel glue applied with squeeze bottle

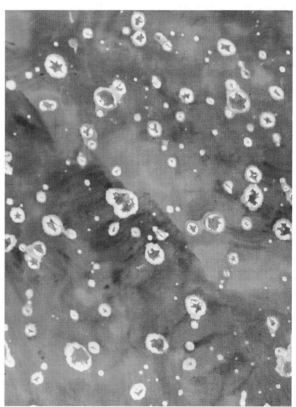

Potato dextrin applied by dripping from spoon

Tip

Use a vanishing marker to draw the design onto the fabric. These markers, available at fabric stores, have ink that washes out in water or disappears on its own.

4. After the resist has dried, follow the directions for applying color and washing out the fabric in Applying Color (page 60–68).

Tip

When creating a detailed design on a lightweight silk, stretch the silk on a wooden stretcher. Use a canvas stretcher, a needlepoint stretcher, a silk-screen frame, or any wooden frame. Use pushpins to attach the silk to the frame: Start on one side and pin an edge of the fabric to one side of the frame. Place the pushpins 1"–2" apart. Then pull the fabric taut and pin the opposite end to the other side of the frame. Pin the remaining sides, keeping the fabric pulled as tightly as possible.

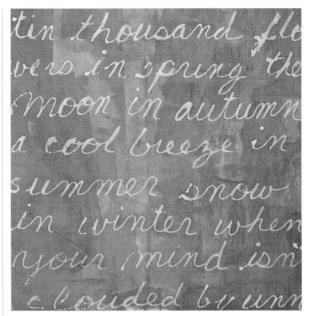

Water-based resist applied with squeeze bottle

Squeeze-Bottle Variation

Create interesting patterns by dragging objects through the resist after it has been squeezed onto the fabric. Try scraping the surface with a notched spreader, a natural-bristle brush, a palette knife, a kitchen scrubber, or some other tool.

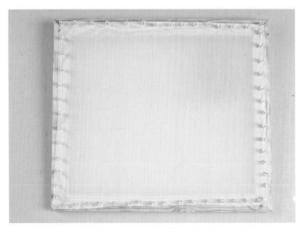

Stretch lightweight fabric on wooden frame before applying resist.

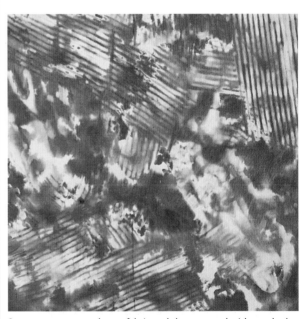

Sugar syrup squeezed onto fabric and then scraped with notched spreader; fabric painted while wet

Stencil

Refer to The Resists (pages 12–35) as needed.

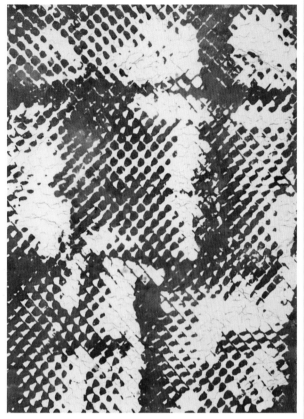

Potato dextrin applied through plastic gutter guard

Applying the resist through a stencil is an easy way to get a clean-edged design on cloth. Stencils are available in a wide range of designs. They are also very easy to make. The advantage to designing them is that you create unique imagery that defines your personal style.

You can use a file folder to make a stencil, but stencil film provides a longer-lasting stencil. The transparent plastic allows you to place the design under the film and trace it. After the design has been transferred to the stencil material, cut out the pattern with a craft knife. If you are using cardboard, paint it with acrylic craft paint before using it, to help it withstand the moisture from the resists.

The stencil technique works well with all the resists except oatmeal.

Make stencils from plastic or cardboard.

> ### Tip
>
> *When making your own stencils, leave at least 1½"
> of stencil material on all sides of the design. This
> provides a place to put the resist without it getting
> on the fabric.*

Materials

- Natural-fiber fabric
- Pins
- Resist of choice
- Plastic spoon
- Stencils
- Small scraper or squeegee
- Bristle brush (1"–3" flat brush, depending on size of fabric)
- MX fiber-reactive dyes

Optional:
- Found objects to use as stencils (such as sequin waste, lace, or construction fencing)

Technique

1. Pin the fabric to the work surface at 6"–8" intervals or use masking tape to adhere the edges.

2. Prepare the resist (pages 12–35).

3. Place a small amount of the resist onto an edge of the stencil. If the image on the stencil is less than an inch from the edge of the stencil, place a piece of thin cardboard on top of the fabric, just above the stencil, to prevent the resist from bleeding onto the fabric.

Apply spoonful of resist to edge of stencil.

4. Use the scraper to pull the resist across the surface of the stencil. The resist will sink into the spaces left by the holes in the stencil. Take care not to allow the resist to flow over the edges of the stencil.

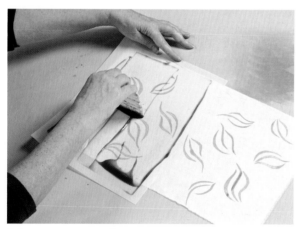

Pull scraper across stencil.

> ### Tip
> Make sure the width of the scraper is narrower than the width of the stencil.

5. After the resist has dried, follow the directions for applying color and washing out the fabric in Applying Color (pages 60–68).

Fabric with potato dextrin applied through stencil

Fabric with corn dextrin applied through stencil

Stencil Variation

An alternative to commercial or homemade stencils is to use found objects as stencils. Any item that is flat and fairly thin and has openings can be used as a stencil. For example, sequin waste, some types of lace, construction fencing, and produce netting can be used as stencils. These will typically result in a more abstracted image and are a great way to create a background texture. Place the item on top of the fabric and apply the resist as described above, or use a brush to apply the resist.

Household objects make great stencils.

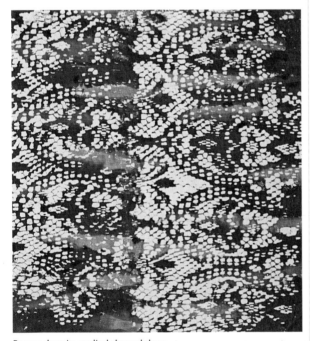

Potato dextrin applied through lace

Water-based resist brushed through mesh laundry bag

Tip

Paint both sides of lace with acrylic paint to stiffen it so it is easier to work with. Heavier or open-weave lace tends to work better than very thin, fine lace.

Stamp

Refer to The Resists (pages 12–35) as needed.

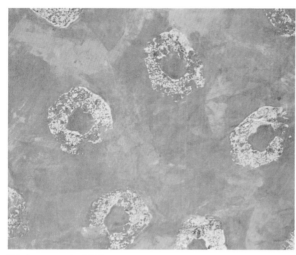

Fabric stamped with flour paste

Sponges make excellent stamps for applying many of the resists. They absorb a great deal and can be stamped several times without reloading. Sponges can easily be cut into just about any shape with scissors. Another wonderful tool is the compressed sponge. It comes as a flat sheet that can be cut with scissors or a utility knife. When it is placed in water, it expands to its normal size. Stamping works with all the resists except oatmeal. Sugar, potato and corn dextrin, acrylic medium, and water-based resists are particularly effective when stamped.

Sponge stamps

Materials

♦ Natural-fiber fabric
♦ Pins
♦ Resist of choice
♦ Sponges
♦ Plastic spoon
♦ Acrylic sheet or flat palette
♦ Bristle brush (1"–3" flat brush, depending on size of fabric)
♦ MX fiber-reactive dyes

Optional:

♦ Leaves
♦ Items to use as stamps (such as kitchen scrubber, metal hardware items, or potato masher)

Technique

1. Pin the fabric to the work surface at 6"–8" intervals or use masking tape to adhere the edges.

2. Prepare the resist (pages 12–35).

3. Pour a small amount of the resist onto an acrylic sheet or other flat surface. Lightly dab the sponge into the resist and then onto a clean space on the acrylic sheet to remove excess resist. Press the stamp onto the fabric. Repeat as needed to create the desired pattern.

Lightly dab stamp into resist; dab off excess on acrylic plate.

Press stamp onto fabric.

> **Tip**
>
> *When working with a cellulose sponge, wet the sponge and then squeeze out the excess water before stamping. This softens the sponge, making it easier to stamp.*

4. After the resist has dried, follow the directions for applying color and washing out the fabric in Applying Color (pages 60–68).

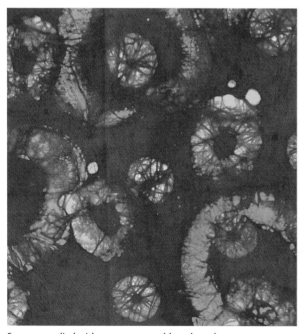

Soy wax applied with sponge stamp (three layers)

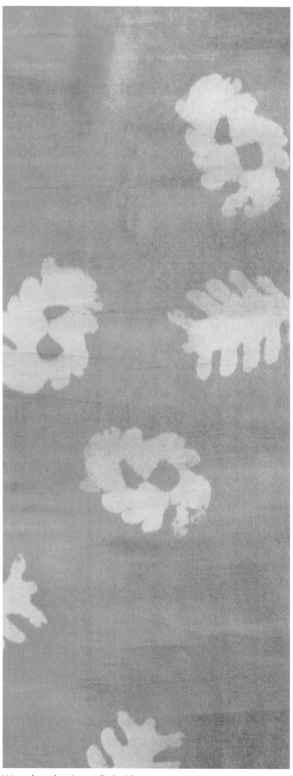

Water-based resist applied with sponge stamp

2. Apply a thin coating of the resist to the back of a leaf with a pouncer or foam roller.

Apply resist to leaf with foam roller.

3. Place the leaf, resist side down, on the fabric. Place a piece of paper or scrap cloth on top of the leaf and press down with your fingers or roll over it with a brayer.

Cover leaf with scrap paper and press down on top of leaf.

4. After the resist has dried, follow the directions for applying color and washing out the fabric in Applying Color (pages 60–68).

> ## *Tip*
>
> *When working with soy wax, use a thick sponge such as a car-washing sponge. The extra thickness will keep your fingers out of the wax! Let the excess wax drip off the sponge into the wax pot. This will result in a clearer image. Too much wax will make a big blob and will be difficult to wash out.*

Thick car-washing sponges are ideal for use with soy wax.

Stamp Variations

LEAF PRINT

Go to the source—use real leaves rather than a manufactured leaf stamp. Look for leaves with distinctive shapes and dimensional veins. Follow the steps below for successful leaf printing.

1. Choose fresh leaves, not dried leaves that have been lying on the ground for a while. Press the leaves between the pages of a book overnight. Flat leaves are easier to work with and make a clearer print.

Water-based resist leaf print

Tip

Don't limit yourself to just leaf prints; other plant parts can be used to dab or brush on resists. The end of a rosemary bush makes an interesting pattern when dabbed onto the fabric.

COMMERCIAL STAMPS AND FOUND OBJECTS

Some commercial stamps will work with resists. Look for bold designs rather than fine-lined images. The wooden tjaps used for batik work well with most of the resists. As with stencils, I also encourage you to make your own stamps or use everyday objects to create a design that is exclusively yours. Look for items with interesting shapes, such as a potato masher, aluminum kitchen scrubbers, or metal hardware items. To apply the resist with these items, use the same technique as for sponge stamps (page 48).

Found objects make great stamps.

Tip

If an object has a lot of nooks and crannies, lightly dab the resist onto the stamp instead of pressing the stamp directly into the resist. If the crevices become filled with the resist, the stamped image will be blurry and messy.

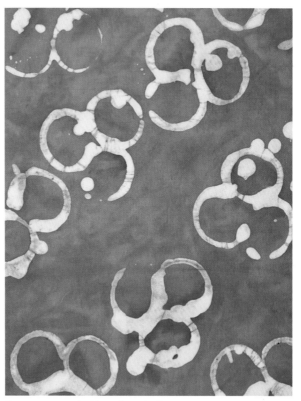

Soy wax stamped with cardboard tubes

Screen Print

Refer to The Resists (pages 12–35) as needed.

Acrylic medium and water-based resist screen print

Screen printing is one of the best ways to get a detailed image onto cloth. It provides an even application of the resist, and you can put just about any image on the silkscreen. Thermofax and PhotoEZ are newer alternatives to traditional wooden silkscreens.

Screens to print resists onto fabric

Screen printing is best suited to acrylic medium, commercial resists, and corn and potato dextrin. The organic pastes, such as flour and oatmeal, will not penetrate the silkscreen, so they leave only a faint residual resist.

Preparing a Wooden Silkscreen

You can buy wooden silkscreens from most art supply stores, some craft stores, and on the Internet (see Resources, page 94). Look for a mesh size of 10xx or 110. A higher number indicates a finer weave, which may make it more difficult for the resist to penetrate.

Before using the frame, scrub the mesh with powdered bathtub cleanser and rinse thoroughly to remove all traces of the cleanser. Then treat the wood with a few coats of varnish or completely cover the wood with duct tape. This will prevent the wood from warping. If the wood is varnished, place strips of duct tape on the inside edges of the screen, overlapping the edge of the mesh by ¾". This creates a "well" in which to put the thickened dye.

Apply duct tape to inside edges of screen to form well.

There are a variety of ways to put an image on a silkscreen, including photo emulsion, screen filler, and hand painting a design. Although a complete description of these processes is beyond the scope of this book, there are many resources available on creating a silkscreen (see Resources, page 94).

CREATING A MASK

Create your own designs on a silkscreen by creating a mask with masking tape, freezer paper, or frisket film. Masking tape is best for simple geometric designs or torn shapes. Freezer paper is available at most grocery stores and craft stores. One side is shiny and can be temporarily adhered to the fabric by ironing. It works well for bold designs. Frisket film is a clear plastic film with a temporary adhesive on one side. It is the better alternative for creating a design with intricate details.

Or lightly iron freezer paper to screen.

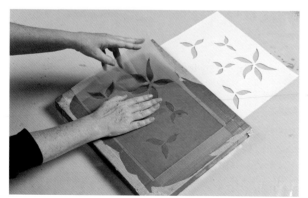

Cut or tear masking tape into desired shape and adhere to back of silkscreen.

Draw design onto frisket film or freezer paper. Cut with craft knife.

Press frisket film to back of silkscreen.

Tip

Tape the freezer-paper stencil to the back of the screen with masking tape and then turn the screen over and iron from the inside of the screen. Take care not to let the iron touch the duct tape on the screen.

Alternatives to a Wooden Silkscreen

THERMOFAX SCREEN

A special machine and plastic film are required to create a Thermofax screen. They are very easy to make from a photocopy of an image. If you do not have a Thermofax machine, use one of the many Thermofax services to have a screen made (see Resources, page 94). The main limitation to the Thermofax is the size. The standard size is 8″ × 10″, although some machines allow for a slightly larger screen.

PHOTOEZ SCREEN

This type of screen is similar to a photo emulsion silk-screen, except that it requires no special chemicals or equipment. The light-sensitive emulsion is already on the mesh. Just place a photocopy of the image under the screen and expose it to sunlight. Once exposed and washed, the mesh can be taped to a plastic Thermofax frame. The screen comes in 8½″ × 11″ sheets and in larger 11″ × 17″ rolls.

Detailed information on how to prepare a PhotoEZ screen is available on the manufacturer's website (see Resources, page 94).

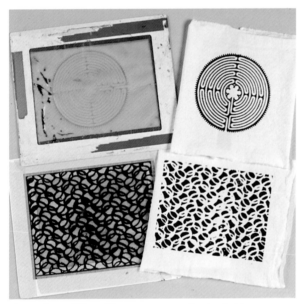

Thermofax and PhotoEZ screens are great for detailed images.

Materials

♦ Natural-fiber fabric

♦ Pins

♦ Resist of choice (acrylic medium or water-based resist)

♦ Plastic spoon

♦ Screen for printing (wooden silkscreen, Thermofax, or PhotoEZ film)

♦ Squeegee or scraper appropriate for silkscreen (see page 55 for more information)

♦ Bristle brush (1″–3″ flat brush, depending on size of fabric)

♦ MX fiber-reactive dyes

Technique

1. Pin the fabric to the work surface at 3″–4″ intervals or use masking tape to adhere the edges. Pull the fabric taut when pinning or taping.

2. Prepare the resist (pages 12–35).

3. Place a small amount of the resist along an edge of the silkscreen.

Apply resist along edge of screen or Thermofax.

4. Use the squeegee to pull the resist across the surface of the screen.

Pull squeegee across screen.

Squeegees and Scrapers

Use a squeegee that is sized to the screen. Use a Speedball fabric squeegee for a wooden silkscreen—the rounded edge is designed specifically for use on fabric and the plastic handle makes it lightweight. Use a smaller squeegee or scraper for a Thermofax or PhotoEZ screen. Sources for scrapers include Bondo spreaders available at auto supply stores, adhesive spreaders from home improvement stores, and 4″ plastic squeegees available from art supply stores.

Use proper squeegee for screen.

5. After the resist has dried, follow the directions for applying color and washing out the fabric in Applying Color (pages 60–68).

Potato dextrin screen print

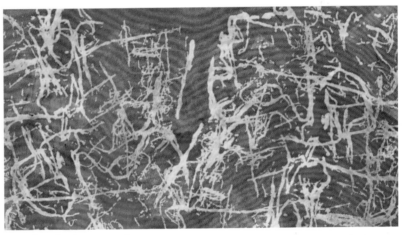

Water-based resist screen print

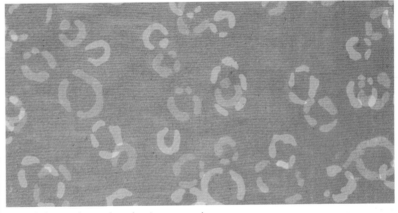

Multiple layers of water-based resist screen print

Brayer Print

Refer to The Resists (pages 12–35) as needed.

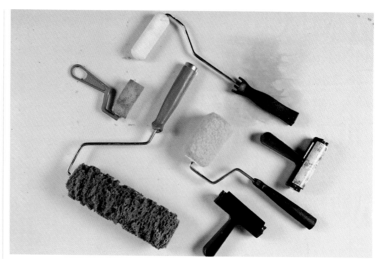
Brayers

Corn dextrin applied with brayer

Materials

♦ Natural-fiber fabric
♦ Pins
♦ Resist of choice
♦ Plastic spoon
♦ Plexiglas plate or flat plastic tray
♦ Brayer or foam roller
♦ Flat, textured objects to place under fabric (such as straw place mats, sink mats, corrugated cardboard, trivets, or rubber bands)
♦ Bristle brush (1"–3" flat brush, depending on size of fabric)
♦ MX fiber-reactive dyes

Optional:
♦ Variety of other brayers and rollers (including rubber brayers, wall painting rollers, and textured rollers)

Applying the resists with a brayer is a great way to add background pattern—textured items are placed underneath the cloth, and the resist is applied on top using a brayer. This technique is suitable for all the resists except oatmeal. Soy wax cannot be applied with a brayer either; however, you can place textured items under the cloth and apply wax lightly with a brush to achieve a similar effect.

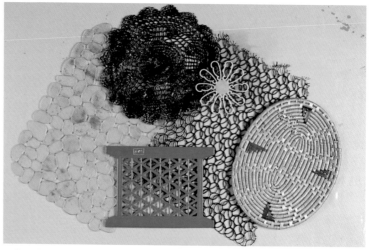
Collect flat items with texture to place under fabric.

Technique

1. Lay the textured item flat on the work surface.

2. Place the fabric on top of the textured item and pin it to the work surface at 3″–4″ intervals or use masking tape to adhere the edges.

Place textured items under fabric.

3. Prepare the resist (pages 12–25).

4. Spoon a small amount of the resist onto the Plexiglas plate. Spread the resist evenly over the plate with a brayer. The goal is to have an even coating of the resist on the brayer surface.

Apply spoonful of resist to Plexiglas plate; roll brayer over resist to get even coating.

Tip

Do not apply too much resist to the Plexiglas plate. A heavy coating will not produce a clean image. The amount of resist needed varies greatly depending on the type of brayer and the resist being used.

5. Lightly roll the brayer over the fabric. It may take a little practice to determine the right amount of pressure to put on the brayer. Roll in one direction to obtain a clearer image.

Roll brayer over fabric.

Tip

The Speedball black foam brayer is a great all-purpose brayer that works well with all resists. If you have only one, that is the one to have.

6. Repeat Steps 4 and 5 until the entire surface of the cloth is patterned. Move the textured item as needed.

7. After the resist has dried, follow the directions for applying color and washing out the fabric in Applying Color (pages 60–68).

Potato dextrin brayer-printed over plastic grid

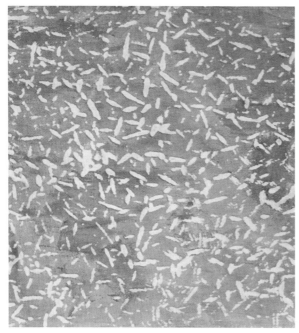

Water-based resist brayer-printed over straw place mat

Corn dextrin brayer-printed over bubble wrap

Brayer Printing Variations

- Try the brayer technique without any textured items underneath the cloth, letting the brayer create the pattern.

- Try using both foam and rubber brayers. Each brayer creates a different pattern.

- Experiment with some of the various napped and faux texture paint rollers available in home improvement stores.

- Another variation is to use masking tape or freezer paper to block off parts of the fabric. Then apply the resist over the entire cloth with a brayer to create the design.

Corn dextrin brayer print with ½" napped roller

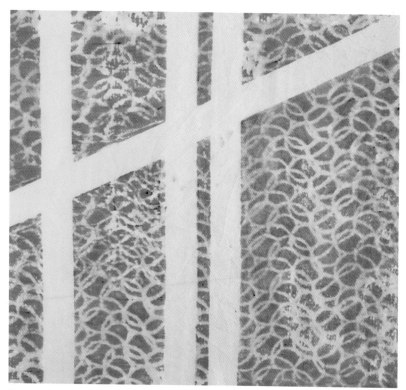

Brayer print over masked fabric

Applying Color

Dyes versus Paints

Both dyes and paints can be used with the resist techniques, but I prefer to use dyes for several reasons.

♦ Dyes produce brilliant color and leave no stiffness on the fabric. Even the best textile paints affect the drape and hand of very sheer fabrics.

♦ MX fiber-reactive dyes do not require heat setting or steaming. The process of pressing or steaming can have an adverse effect on some resists.

About Fiber-Reactive Dyes

MX dyes and auxiliary chemicals required

There are several types of fiber-reactive dyes. I use Procion type MX fiber-reactive dyes. These dyes come in a powdered form and are considered nontoxic. Formulated in the mid-1950s, these dyes are very easy to use, they produce vibrant colors, and they are very washfast and lightfast. The dye forms a chemical bond with the fiber molecules, making the color permanent.

After the dyes have been applied, they need to "batch." Batching simply means to let the fabric sit while moist so the dyes have time to react with the fiber molecules.

Several things are required for this chemical bond to occur:

♦ Sodium carbonate (also called soda ash) produces the alkaline conditions necessary for the chemical reaction to take place.

♦ The fabric must be moist in order for the reaction to occur. After the fabric dries, the reaction stops, which can lead to paler colors. The recipes below contain urea, which is a humectant. It draws in moisture to keep the cloth damp while the reaction takes place.

♦ Time and temperature are two other variables that play an important role when working with MX dyes. The dyes need 4–24 hours for the chemical bond to take place. The ideal room temperature for batching is 75°F or higher. A longer batching time is needed if the room temperature is cooler.

♦ MX dyes work only on cellulose and protein fibers, so synthetic fabrics such as nylon, polyester, or acetate will not take the dye.

The dyes are offered in a variety of colors and can be mixed to create your own personalized palette. MX dyes and the auxiliary chemicals are available at some art supply stores and through many Internet retailers (see Resources, page 94). Soda ash is also available at most pool supply stores.

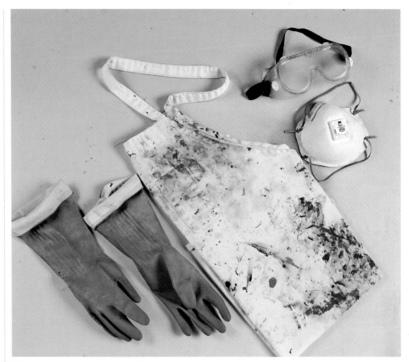
Wear protective gear when using dyes.

Safety Guidelines

Although MX dyes are considered nontoxic and safe to use, some safety precautions are in order.

♦ Always wear a dust mask when working with soda ash and the dyes in their powdered state. Soda ash is a caustic substance that can irritate the respiratory system. Continued breathing of the powdered dyes can cause allergies or respiratory problems. After the dyes and soda ash are mixed in a solution with water, a dust mask is not necessary.

♦ Always wear rubber gloves when working with the dyes.

♦ After a container or tool has been used with dyes, never use it for food mixing or food storage.

♦ Do not mix dyes in an area that is used for food preparation.

Hand Painting with Dye

Refer to Applying the Resists (pages 36–59) as needed.

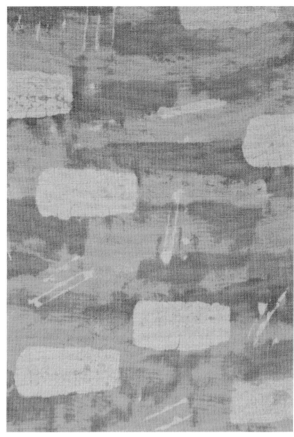

Hand painting over potato dextrin applied with sponge and wire whisk

Thickened dyes work best for hand painting over most resists because liquid dyes without any thickener dissolve the resists more easily. The main exception to this is when using the wet-on-wet technique (page 65). In that case, liquid dyes blend better than thickened dyes. Use the recipe given for the low water immersion method (page 67) if you are hand painting with liquid dyes.

Sodium alginate, a substance derived from seaweed, is used to thicken dyes for hand painting. It comes in a high viscosity / low solids (SH) version and a low viscosity / high solids (F) version. Typically the F is recommended for silk and the SH for cotton, but for our uses the SH version will work on any fabric type.

Dye Thickener

- ◆ ¼ cup urea
- ◆ 1 quart hot water
- ◆ 2 tablespoons sodium alginate

1. Place the urea in a quart-size container. Add the water and stir until dissolved.

2. Sprinkle the sodium alginate slowly into the water, stirring continuously. A wire whisk or handheld blender works best for blending in the sodium alginate, *or* mix this in a blender dedicated to studio use.

Sprinkle sodium alginate into water and blend.

3. Allow the mixture to sit for several hours or overnight to thicken.

A consistency similar to pancake syrup works well, but the recipe can be adjusted to suit individual needs. A very thin mixture will create more bleeding, resulting in less definition and more dye color on the surface. A thicker mixture will result in a crisper line and less dye color on the fabric. The thickness of the fabric will also affect the results.

Also keep in mind that sodium alginate is an organic substance and therefore is not standardized from batch to batch. Tweak the recipe to obtain the thickness you prefer. This mixture will last several months in the refrigerator.

Preparing the Thickened Dye Mixture

- ½ cup dye thickener
- ⅛ to ½ teaspoon dye powder, depending on depth of color desired
- ½ teaspoon soda ash

1. Add the dye powder to the thickener and stir until dissolved.

2. Add the soda ash and stir well.

Add dye powder and soda ash to thickener; stir well.

Tips

Mix up just the amount needed, as this mixture will last only 3–4 hours. After that time, the dye will have reacted with the soda ash and will leave little color on the fabric.

Some dyes dissolve more easily than others. If the dye is not completely dissolved before it is used for painting, it may leave streaks of color on the fabric. To avoid this, let the dye powder and thickener mixture sit for 10–15 minutes before adding the soda ash.

Bring the thickener to room temperature before adding the dye and soda ash. Stir immediately after adding the soda ash; otherwise, it can form clumps that will not dissolve.

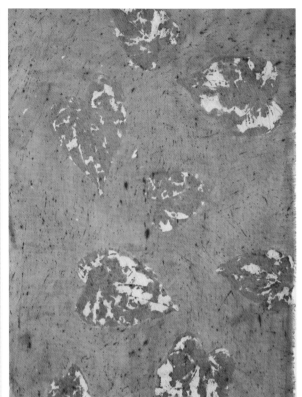

Red specks in background indicate that dye was not completely dissolved.

Painting with Thickened Dye

1. Pin the fabric to the work surface.

2. Mix the thickened dye (at left).

3. Use a brush, scraper, spatula, sponge, or blank silkscreen to apply the dye.

Use 2"–3" flat brush to paint on dye.

Small scraper or old credit card can also be used to apply thickened dye.

This cloth was batched in plastic—note how dye breached resist.

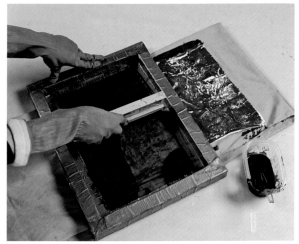

Pull thickened dye through blank silkscreen to get even coating of color.

4. Cover the fabric with an old sheet and let sit for 12–24 hours.

> ### Tip
>
> *A fabric sheet on the work surface is preferable to plastic for batching, to reduce the chance of the dye penetrating the resist. Unless you are working in an extremely dry environment, plastic will keep the fabric too damp. However, use plastic to achieve a more marbled effect.*

> ### Tip
>
> *Paste resists can be hard on brushes, so use inexpensive brushes to apply the dye. Synthetic-bristle brushes work very well for applying dye. They have more spring and are easier to work with than natural-bristle brushes.*

Painting with Liquid Dye

1. Pin the fabric to the work surface.

2. Mix the dyes (page 67).

3. Use a brush or an eyedropper to apply the dye. When brushing on liquid dyes, wipe the brush against the side of the dye container to remove excess dye. This helps prevent flooding the fabric with dye, thus breaching the resist.

4. Cover the fabric in an old sheet and let sit for 12–24 hours.

5. Wash out the resist and dye (page 68).

Low Water Immersion Dyeing

Refer to Applying the Resists (pages 36–59) as needed.

Many of the resists can be used in an immersion dye bath. A full immersion dye bath would not be suitable for most of the resists, since most of them are water soluble. In low water immersion, a small amount of dye is poured over the fabric. Leave the fabric sitting in the excess dye for a softer effect with more dye penetrating the resist. Pour off the excess dye for a crisper edge with less dye penetration. Either approach can yield satisfactory results.

Tip

If you are using a resist that you mix yourself, make a thicker version if you plan to immerse the cloth, or use a heavier application of the resist. This will help it hold up longer.

Mixing the Dye

- 1 teaspoon soda ash
- ¼ to 1 teaspoon dye powder, depending on depth of color desired
- 1 cup warm water (90°–100°F)

Place the soda ash and dye in a small plastic container. Add a small amount of the water. Stir until dissolved. Add the remaining water and stir well.

Tip

If you are working with soy wax, allow the dye to cool slightly before pouring it over the fabric. The wax is less likely to soften that way. Another option is to leave the cloth in the refrigerator or freezer for about 20 minutes before placing it in the dye. This will harden the wax so it will resist better.

Applying the Dye

1. Place the fabric in a flat plastic container. The container should be large enough so that the fabric will fit with a minimum of scrunching.

2. Pour the dye over the fabric, making sure to reach all areas of the cloth.

Pour dye over fabric.

3. Let the fabric batch for 4–24 hours. The longer the batch time, the more likely it is that the dye will penetrate the resist. The container does not need to be covered unless it is in a very dry environment.

4. Wash as directed below.

Acrylic medium, immersed

Washing Out the Resist and Dye

1. Once the fabric has batched, soak it in warm water for 15–20 minutes to soften the resist.

2. Rinse the fabric, rubbing with a scrub brush if necessary to remove excess resist.

3. Wash the fabric in the washing machine with hot water and ½ teaspoon Synthrapol to remove all excess dye and resist.

4. Dry in the dryer or hang to dry. Some resists may leave the fabric slightly stiff. Use a fabric softener, if necessary, to reduce stiffness.

Tip

Before placing the fabric in the dryer, make sure all the resist residue has been removed. If any resist remains on the fabric, wash or rinse it again. The resists can be difficult to remove once they are exposed to the heat of the dryer.

Resist-Specific Wash-Out Tips

SOY WAX

Soy wax removal requires a water temperature of at least 140°F. If you keep your hot water heater set to a lower temperature, temporarily turn it up for the washout or add some boiling water to the machine as it fills. Add a small amount of Synthrapol to the water to help remove the wax. If the wax is difficult to remove, use a wash setting with two rinse cycles or soak the fabric in hot water for 15 minutes before placing it in the washing machine.

FLOUR, OATMEAL, AND POTATO DEXTRIN

A bit of scrubbing may be required to completely remove these resists. The thickness of the paste and the weave of the fabric will determine how easily the resist comes off. A thin coating of paste will generally dissolve in warm water. A thicker application of paste may require a gentle

rubbing with a scrub brush to loosen the paste. These resists can come off in large chunks, which may clog the drain. Either pour off the residue outside or strain the solid contents and place them in the trash.

Use scrub brush if necessary to remove resist.

Tip

An outdoor hose with a spray nozzle is ideal for washing off excess flour, oatmeal, or potato dextrin. Place the cloth flat on a table and spray it with water. Scrub gently with a brush to remove stubborn pieces of the resist.

COMMERCIAL WATER-BASED RESISTS, CORN DEXTRIN, AND SUGAR

These resists tend to be a bit sticky, and a little rubbing may be needed to completely remove them.

ACRYLIC MEDIUM

Acrylic medium will not wash out of the fabric, so it does not need to be soaked in warm water. A short soak in cold water before placing the fabric in the washing machine will help remove some of the excess dye.

Layering the Techniques

If one resist is good, two are even better! Use multiple techniques on the same piece of cloth to create a surface rich with depth and texture.

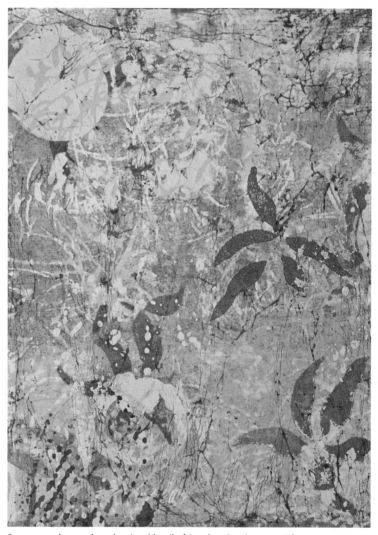

Soy wax and water-based resists (detail of *Bamboo Sunrise*, page 79)

General Guidelines

In most cases, wash the fabric before adding each successive layer. This is true for any of the crackle techniques and the more easily dissolved resists, such as potato and corn dextrin and sugar syrup. When using wax, you do not need to wash it out between layers. Leaving the wax in the cloth can yield very interesting results because each layer of wax will continue to resist additional layers of dye. The main caveat is that the sodium alginate in thickened dye acts as a resist, so additional layers of dye will not penetrate previous layers very well. It is best to immerse the fabric or hand paint it with thin dyes.

The crackle and sgraffito techniques are great as a first layer. They create a wonderful backdrop that goes with anything. Additional layers can be composed of additional resists applied with any of the other application techniques.

One approach is to use the same tool with a different resist on each layer. Or use the same image in different sizes for each layer. For example, if you carved a sponge stamp for soy wax, make a smaller version of the stamp and use it with potato dextrin for the next layer. Then make a stencil with the same image and use it with a commercial water-based resist for the third layer.

Sample Ideas

The possibilities for layering are limited only by your imagination—pretty much anything goes. Here are a few suggested approaches to get you started. Refer to Applying the Resists (pages 36–59) and Applying Color (pages 60–68) as needed.

Soy Wax Times 3

1. Apply soy wax using the tool of your choice. Allow the wax to cool.

2. Immerse the cloth in dye or hand paint the fabric with thin dyes, batch, rinse in cool water, and line dry. Do not rinse in warm water or wash the fabric. The idea is to keep the wax intact for subsequent layers. Use a shorter batch time for this technique (2–3 hours). That will help prevent the wax from degrading from the water and soda ash.

3. Apply another layer of soy wax, using the same or a different tool. Allow the wax to cool.

4. Immerse in dye, batch, rinse in cool water, and line dry.

5. Repeat Steps 1 and 2 if desired.

6. Wash out the resist and dye.

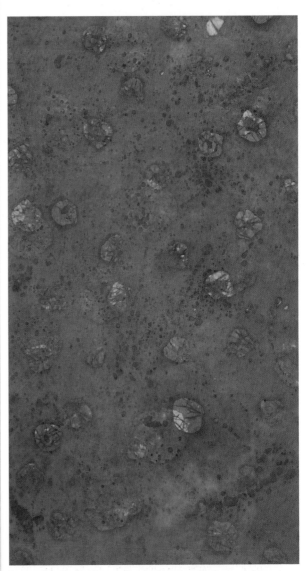

Soy wax applied in three layers and immersed after each layer

Ghost Image

1. Apply textile medium to the fabric with a silkscreen or stencil. Let it dry.

2. Use the same silkscreen or stencil to apply a water-based resist. Let it dry.

3. Using 2–3 coordinated colors of dye, immerse or hand paint the fabric with thickened dye. Batch and wash.

4. Repeat Steps 1–3 if desired.

Lighter, ghostlike images were printed with acrylic medium; more colorful images were printed with water-based resist and took on color of subsequent dyeing.

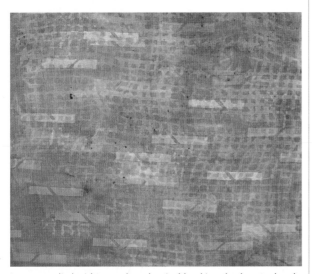

Images applied with water-based resist blend into background and are barely visible.

Crackle Plus

1. Apply flour paste, potato dextrin, or oatmeal over the surface of the cloth.

2. Allow the resist to dry, scrunch the fabric to crack the paste, and hand paint with dye. Batch, wash, and dry.

3. Apply soy wax, a water-based resist, or corn dextrin with a bold stamped image.

4. Hand paint or immerse the cloth. Batch, wash, and dry.

5. Apply a different resist using an image that complements the first 2 layers. Stamp, stencil, or screen-print a design, or just apply the resist with a brush or other tool. Allow it to dry.

6. Hand paint or immerse the cloth. Batch, wash, and dry.

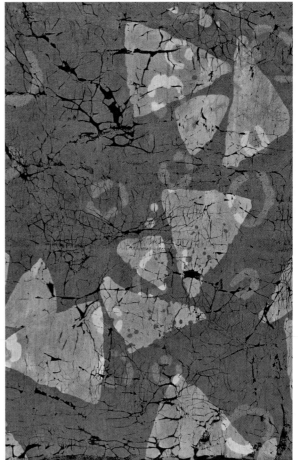

Flour paste crackle, soy wax stamp, and water-based resist screen-print

One Tool

1. Apply any of the resists with a sponge stamp or stencil. Allow it to dry.

2. Hand paint, batch, and wash.

3. Repeat Steps 1 and 2 twice more, using the same stamp or stencil. Use the same resist each time or choose a different one.

Potato dextrin brushed through plastic grid (three layers)

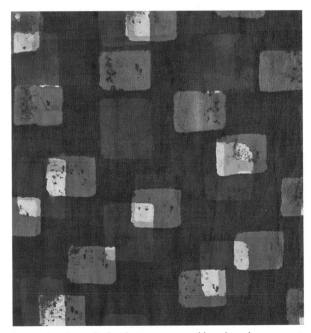

Potato dextrin applied with sponge stamp (three layers)

Flour paste crackle, soy wax stencil, and potato dextrin screen-print

Wet-on-Wet

1. Apply soy wax or acrylic medium in a bold design. Let it dry.

2. Apply flour paste or potato dextrin using the sgraffito technique *or* apply sugar syrup using the squeeze-bottle technique. While the resist is damp, apply dye.

3. Batch, wash, and dry the cloth.

4. Repeat Steps 2 and 3 if desired.

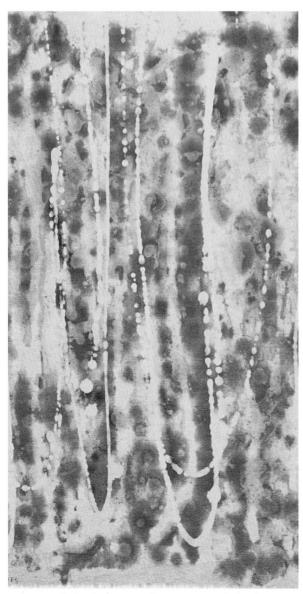

Soy wax applied with tjanting and sugar syrup applied with squeeze bottle; liquid dyes applied with pipette

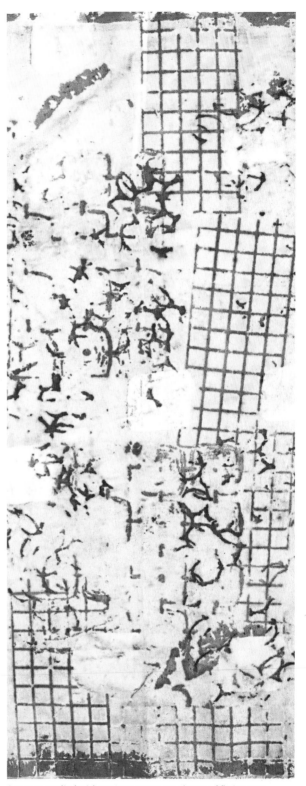

Soy wax applied with sponge stamp, two layers of flour paste applied with sgraffito technique; painted while damp and washed between layers

Fault Line by Lisa Kerpoe, 32″ × 40″, 2011

Silk/soy, potato dextrin resist, multiple layers of hand painting, metal leaf lamination

Photo by Lynn Luukinen

Smart Polly by Linda Rael,
12″ wide × 10″ high × 9″ deep, 2011

Cotton, oatmeal and potato dextrin resist, real parrot skull, hand
and machine stitching, hand beading, embellishment with found
objects; based on a pattern by Abigail Patner Glassenberg in *The
Artful Bird*

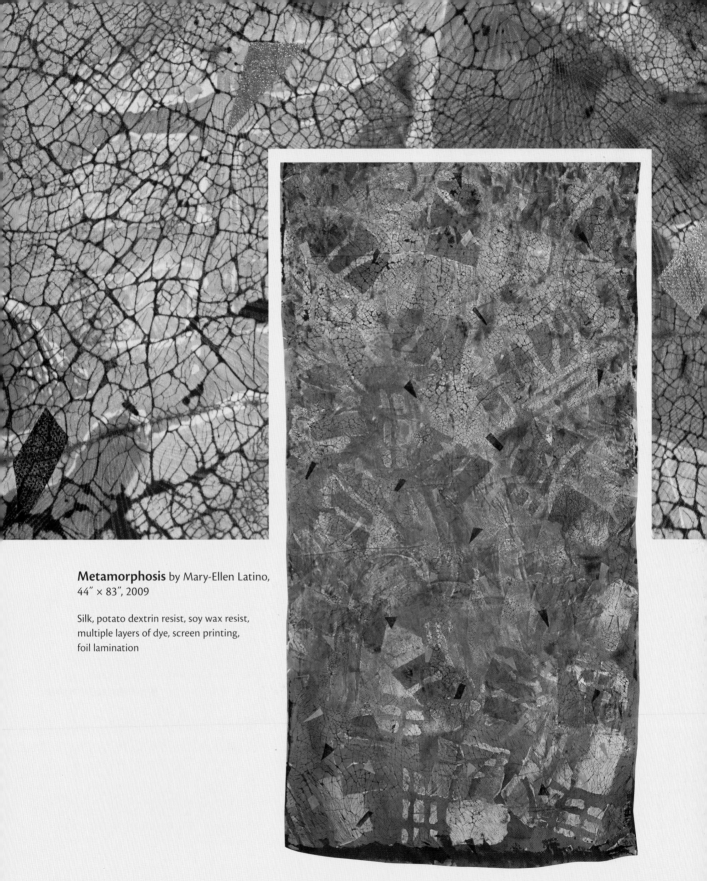

Metamorphosis by Mary-Ellen Latino,
44″ × 83″, 2009

Silk, potato dextrin resist, soy wax resist,
multiple layers of dye, screen printing,
foil lamination

Tree Line by Barbara J. Schneider, detail; finished project 96″ × 96″, 2011

Silk/hemp, soy wax resist, hand painting with dye, stitching, needle felting

Bamboo Sunrise by Lisa Kerpoe, 9″ × 19″, 2009

Cotton, flour paste resist, soy wax resist, water-based resist, screen printing with dye and textile paint, metal leaf lamination

Photo by Ansen Seale

Frostfire by Caryl Gaubatz, 2011

Silk charmeuse and silk organza, flour paste resist, hand painting with dye; made using the
Ikina Jacket pattern from The Sewing Workshop

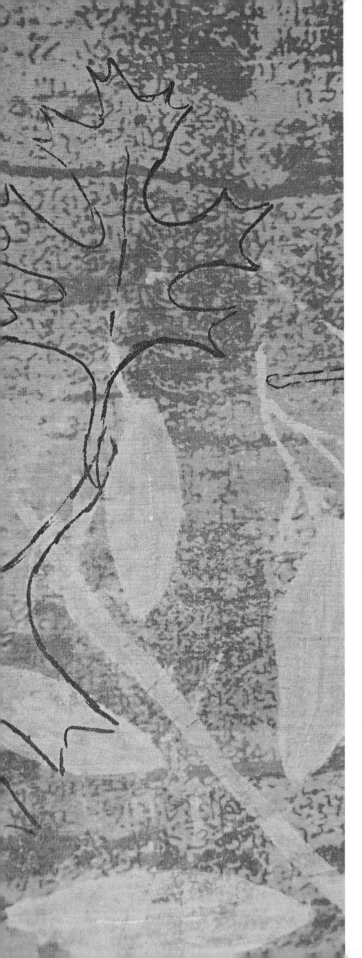

Photo by Lynn Luukinen

Ties to Nature by Lisa Kerpoe, 30″ × 94″, 2009

Silk organza, soy wax resist, water-based resist, multiple layers of screen printing with dye and textile paint, metal leaf lamination

Untitled by Jane Dunnewold, 80" × 44", 2009

Silk noil, flour paste resist, soy wax resist, multiple layers of dye
and discharge, devoré with hand-dyed cotton

A 21st-Century Sampler by Kate Martin,
45″ × 39″, 2010

Silk broadcloth, soy wax resist, hand painting with
dye, stenciling, hand-stitched embroidery and
beading, commercially printed cotton appliqué,
machine quilting

Continuum 6 by Joy Nebo Lavrencik,
54" × 44", 2011

Silk broadcloth, multiple layers of soy wax
resist, multiple layers of screen printing with
thickened dye

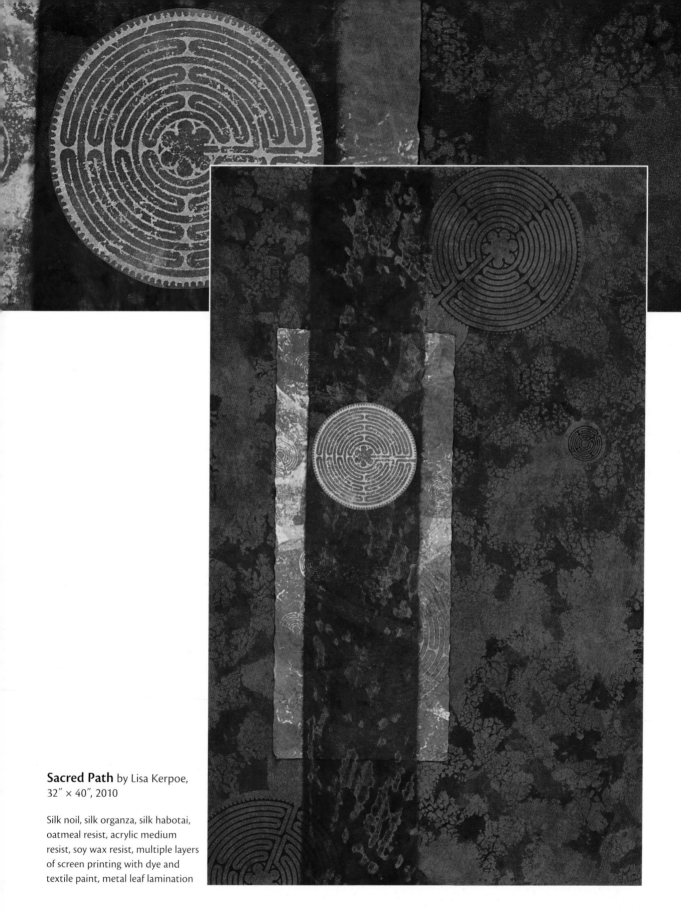

Sacred Path by Lisa Kerpoe,
32″ × 40″, 2010

Silk noil, silk organza, silk habotai,
oatmeal resist, acrylic medium
resist, soy wax resist, multiple layers
of screen printing with dye and
textile paint, metal leaf lamination

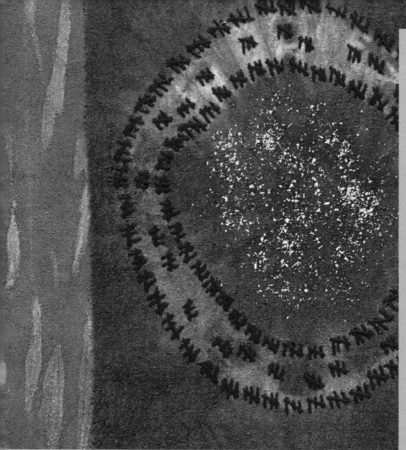

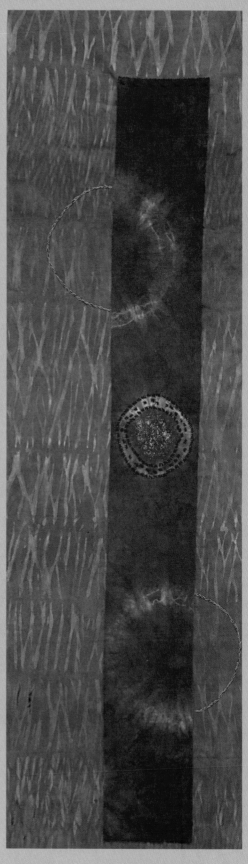

This Moment by Lisa Kerpoe,
24" × 80", 2010

Silk noil, soy wax resist, multiple
layers of dye, hand stitching,
metal leaf lamination

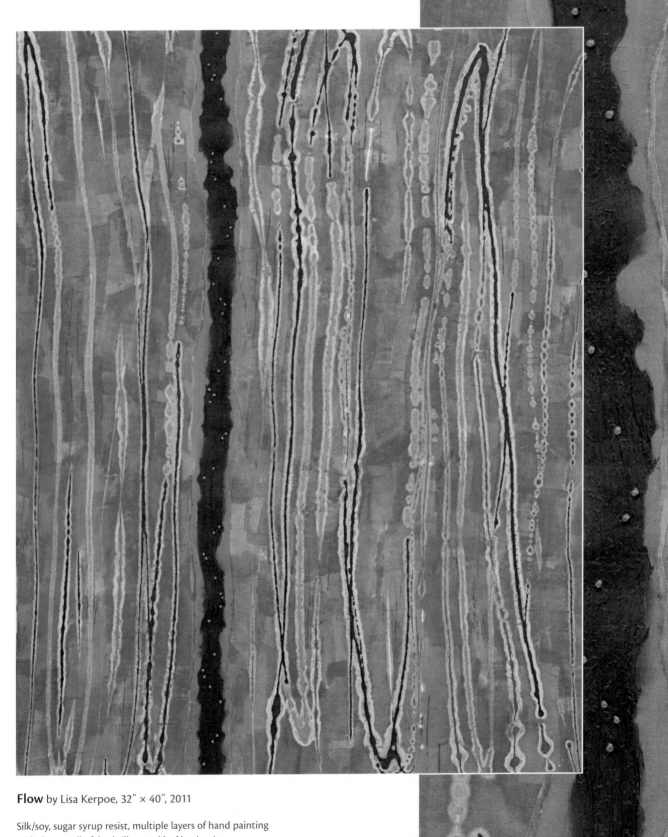

Flow by Lisa Kerpoe, 32″ × 40″, 2011

Silk/soy, sugar syrup resist, multiple layers of hand painting
with dye, needle-felted silk, metal leaf lamination

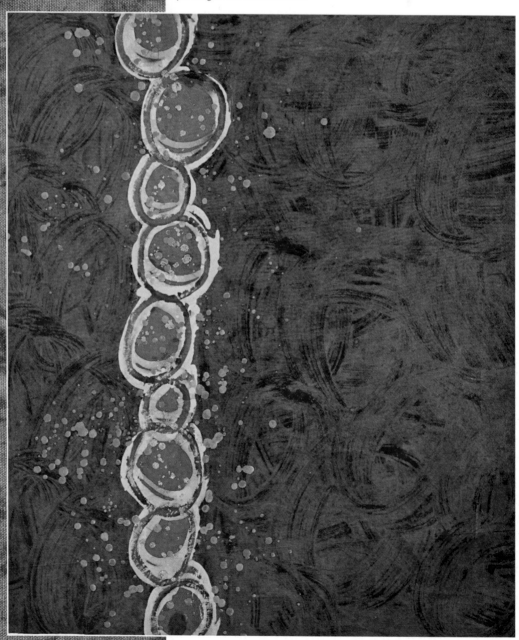

Peace Amidst Chaos by Lisa Kerpoe,
16″ × 20″, 2010

Cotton, soy wax resist, flour paste resist, hand
painting, metal leaf lamination

Awakening by Lisa Kerpoe,
16″ wide × 94″ high × 16″ deep, 2008

Silk organza, acrylic medium resist, water-based resist, multiple layers of screen printing with dye, discharge, metal leaf lamination

Photo by Lynn Luukinen

The Guardians by Lynn Luukinen, 45″ × 96″, 2011

Silk, flour paste resist, potato dextrin resist, soy wax resist, multiple layers of dye, discharge, needle felting, hand stitching

Photo by Lynn Luukinen

The Moon by Lisa Kerpoe,
25″ × 94″, 2010

Linen/rayon, acrylic medium resist,
soy wax resist, multiple layers of dye,
hand painting, hand stitching, metal
leaf lamination

Photo by Lynn Luukinen

Appendix

Troubleshooting Guide

PROBLEM	POSSIBLE CAUSES	SOLUTION
The resist did not wash out completely.	The resist was applied heavily.	After soaking, use a spray hose and/or scrub brush to remove excess resist before placing the fabric in the washing machine.
	The fabric was not soaked before washing.	Soak the fabric for 15–20 minutes in warm water before washing.
	The resist was on the fabric for a long period of time before washing.	Do not allow fabric with a resist to sit for more than a few days. It can be harder to remove the resist—plus it can attract bugs.
The resist will not come out, even after repeated washings.	The fabric had a sizing that reacted with the resist.	Scour the fabric before using the resist (page 11).
The dried oatmeal flaked off the fabric before the dye was applied.	Uncooked resist was used.	Oatmeal requires cooking or hot water to develop the gluten and ensure adhesion.
Dye penetrated the areas with the resist.	The fabric was kept too damp during batching.	Temperature and humidity levels can affect the blocking properties of resists. In humid areas, cover the fabric with a sheet rather than plastic during batching.
	The resist was not dry before dye was applied.	Allow the resist to dry completely before applying dye. If it feels cool to the touch, it may not be fully dry. Drying time will vary based on temperature and humidity.
Very little dye penetrated the cracks in the crackle technique.	The resist was not cracked enough before the fabric was painted with dye.	Squeeze, scrunch, and press the fabric thoroughly after the resist has dried.
	The dye was too thick.	Add a small amount of water to the dye mixture to make it thinner.
The soy wax did not completely block the dye.	The wax was not hot enough to penetrate the fabric.	Make sure the wax is clear when it is applied to the fabric. If it appears opaque, let it heat up more.
	An immersion dye bath was used.	Some penetration of the wax is inevitable with an immersion dye bath. Refer to the tip box Immersion Dyeing with Soy Wax (page 30).
	Inferior-quality or candle-grade wax was used.	Use a wax specifically designed for surface design. Refer to Resources (page 94).
The soy wax did not wash out completely.	The water was not hot enough.	Adjust the temperature on the hot water heater and/or add boiling water to the washing machine to raise the temperature.
	A front-loading washer was used (wax removal may be more difficult because front loaders use very little water).	Soak the fabric in hot water for 15–30 minutes and then rub off the softened wax before placing the fabric in the washing machine.
	The wax was applied heavily.	Soak the fabric in hot water for 15–30 minutes and then rub off the softened wax before placing the fabric in the washing machine.

Recommended Application Techniques for Each Resist

	FLOUR	OATMEAL	POTATO DEXTRIN	CORN DEXTRIN	SUGAR	SOY WAX	ACRYLIC MEDIUM	WATER-BASED RESISTS
Brayer print	Yes	No	Yes	Yes	Yes	No	Yes	Yes
Crackle	Yes	Yes	Yes	No	No	Yes	No	No
Screen print	No	No	Yes	Yes	No	No	Yes	Yes
Sgraffito	Yes	No	Yes	No	No	Yes	No	No
Squeeze bottle	Yes	No	Yes	Yes	Yes	No (use tjanting)	Yes	Yes
Stamp	Yes	No	Yes	Yes	Yes	Yes	Yes	Yes
Stencil	Yes	No	Yes	Yes	Yes	Yes	Yes	Yes

Resources

Dharma Trading Co.
Dyes, paints, resists, fabrics, supplies for stamping and screen printing, clothing blanks
www.dharmatrading.com
800-542-5227

EZ Screenprint
PhotoEZ, other screen-printing supplies
www.ezscreenprint.com
520-423-0409

Grafix
Frisket masking film, stencil film
www.grafixarts.com

Jacquard Products
Jacquard dyes and paints, a variety of fabrics through the company's Silk Connection partner
www.jacquardproducts.com
www.silkconnection.com
800-442-0455

Nasco
Supplies for stamping and screen printing (the company caters to art teachers and has an array of interesting items)
www.enasco.com
800-558-9595

ProChemical and Dye
Dyes, paints, resists, fabric
www.prochemicalanddye.com
800-228-9393

RJR Fabrics
Fabric (mostly prints, but the company carries a very nice dyeable cotton sateen)
www.rjrfabrics.com
800-422-5426

Robert J. Kaufmann
Wide array of PFD fabrics
www.robertkaufman.com
800-877-2066

Test Fabrics
A variety of cotton and rayon fabrics
www.testfabrics.com
570-603-0432

Thai Silks
Silk and silk blend fabrics, clothing and scarf blanks
www.thaisilks.com
800-722-7455

Welsh Products
Screen-printing supplies
www.welshproducts.com
800-745-3255

General information on dyeing
www.pburch.net

Instructions for taping a silkscreen
www.lisakerpoe.com

Information on Thermofaxes
www.maggieweiss.com